ROMANIA

THE ESSENTIAL GUIDE TO CUSTOMS & CULTURE

DEBBIE STOWE

KUPERARD

"The real voyage of discovery consists not in seeking new landscapes, but in having new eyes."

Adapted from Marcel Proust, *Remembrance of Things Past.*

This book is dedicated to the memory of Geoffrey Chesler, founding editor of the Culture Smart! series, whose commitment and vision saw the collection grow to over one hundred country guides. We hope that the fruits of his endeavor toward cross-cultural understanding will continue to inspire readers as they explore new horizons.

ISBN 978 1 78702 382 6

British Library Cataloguing in Publication Data
A CIP catalogue entry for this book is available
from the British Library

First published in Great Britain
by Kuperard, an imprint of Bravo Ltd
59 Hutton Grove, London N12 8DS
Tel: +44 (0) 20 8446 2440
www.culturesmart.co.uk
Inquiries: publicity@kuperard.co.uk

Design Bobby Birchall
Printed in India

ABOUT THE AUTHOR

DEBBIE STOWE is a British author, travel writer, and freelance journalist. A graduate of University College London, and City University, where she studied Periodical Journalism, she is the author of around twenty books. Her many travel guides, for Thomas Cook Publishing, run from the Maldives to Manchester to Mediterranean Cruising. Other published books cover entertainment, celebrity, and the natural world. She has also written first-person, opinion, cultural, social, travel, business, film, and parenting articles for a range of British and international publications, including *Metro* and *The Telegraph*. She lives in Bucharest with her Romanian partner and sons.

CONTENTS

MAP OF ROMANIA

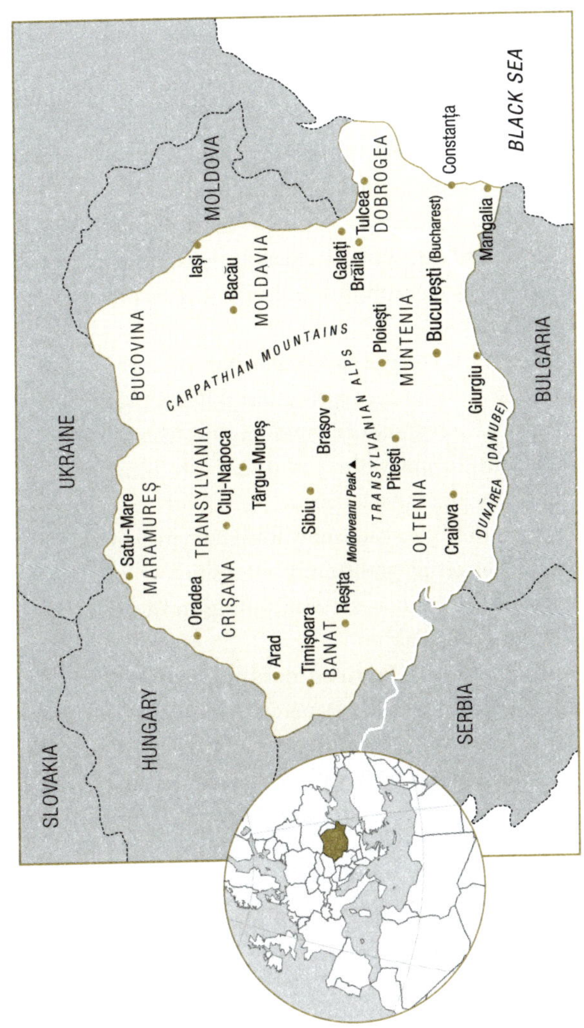

INTRODUCTION

Of all the Eastern European states, Romania probably suffers from the worst reputation, owing mostly to the bleak years of Communism prior to the violent revolution of 1989, then the tragedy of its abandoned children in the 1990s, as well as more recent immigration anxieties. Move beyond the media images, however, or the clichés of Dracula and creepy Transylvanian castles, and you will discover a fascinating, dynamic country that exerts an inexplicable pull even as it frustrates and bewilders you.

Romania's citizens have retained their "seize the day" mentality despite the deprivations and repression of nearly half a century of Communist mismanagement. While their country has rushed zealously to embrace capitalism and conspicuous consumption—a bruising recession and pandemic notwithstanding—they still face the lingering problems of a transition economy, which they bear stoically with a shrug and a resigned "This is Romania."

Culture Smart! Romania looks at the ways the past has shaped present-day Romanian attitudes and behavior. We examine the Latin temperament that sees drivers gesticulating and hooting with a fervor that suggests their manhood depends on it. We meet people at home in the grim Communist-era apartment complexes that they do their best to render cheerful, and into which they will welcome you with the very best of what they have. We study them at work—where some stay late into the night, determined to forge a better life for themselves, while others scroll on their phones while the boss isn't looking—and at play, partying until dawn in basement dives.

Romanian life is not for the fainthearted. The lingering bureaucracy, the occasional curtness, some unenlightened attitudes regarding minorities and science, and patchy infrastructure and services can all be dispiriting. Such drawbacks, however, are more than outweighed by what Romania has to offer. High on the plus side is a marvelous sense of "anything goes." No parking spaces? Leave your car right across the sidewalk. Cell phone ringing during a concert? Just answer it. Feeling amorous in the park? No problem. Running late? Don't worry about it. There's little you can do here that will offend.

Romania also offers great business and career opportunities. Expatriate status still confers respect and authority. Here, an idea that's been done a dozen times back home can still be fairly new to the market. Doing difficult things is simple in Romania (it's the simple things that are difficult to do); and Western money still goes further than back home (pricey coffees in hipster cafés notwithstanding).

But the biggest draw is the warmth of the people, and the wonderful feeling of being in a place where interesting things are happening. If you can negotiate the pitfalls (and we aim to help you do that), you'll discover a place that will continually surprise and challenge you—difficult, sometimes, to live in, but almost impossible to leave.

KEY FACTS

Official Name	Romania (România)	Member of the EU since Jan. 1, 2007
Capital City	Bucharest (București)	Pop. 1.7 million (approx.)
Main Cities	Brașov, Cluj-Napoca, Constanța, Craiova, Galați, Iași, Oradea, Ploiești, Timișoara	
Area	91,699 square miles (237,500 sq. km)	
Borders	Hungary, Moldova, Ukraine, Bulgaria, Serbia	
Climate	Transitional between temperate and continental, with July the hottest month and January the coldest	July temperature averages 70ºF (21.7ºC); January 30ºF (1.1ºC)
Currency	Leu (meaning lion) = 100 bani	Currency code RON
Population	19.7 million	
Ethnic Makeup	Romanian 89.3%, Hungarian 6%, Roma 3.4%, others 1.3%	
Language	Romanian is the main language; Magyar is widely spoken in areas with a high concentration of ethnic Hungarians.	English has now taken over from Russian and French as the main foreign language taught in schools.
Religion	Romanian Orthodox 73.6%, Protestant 6.3%, Roman Catholic 3.9%	Others: Pentecostal, Romanian-Greek Catholic, Muslims, Jews, and atheists

Government	Parliamentary democracy. The head of state is the president, the head of the government the prime minister. The president is elected for a five-year term.	Bicameral parliament consists of the Chamber of Deputies and Senate, both elected every four years under a system of proportional representation.
Romanians Abroad	Diaspora of 6–8 million people	They live mostly in Italy, Spain, Germany, France, and the UK.
Economy	Main exports include: Cars, motor vehicle parts, insulated wire, and wheat. Also a major exporter of sunflower seeds and silk yarn.	Romania's main trading partners are Germany, France, the UK, and Hungary.
Media	Romania's main TV channels include the state-owned public service broadcaster TVR (with channels like TVR1, TVR2, and TVR Cultural), and popular private channels like Pro TV, Antena 1, and Kanal D.	Key English-language publications include *Romania Insider*, *Romania Journal*, and *Bucharest Daily News*, all of which can be accessed online.
Electricity	220 volts, 50 Hz. Continental sockets and plugs	British and American appliances require an adaptor/transformer.
Internet Domain	.ro	
Telephone	Romania's country code is 40.	To dial out, dial 00 then country code.
Time Zone	GMT + 2 hours	Romania has daylight saving time.

CHAPTER **ONE**

LAND & PEOPLE

GEOGRAPHICAL SNAPSHOT

Variously described as being in Eastern and Southeastern Europe, Romania lies just north of the Balkan Peninsula. It can technically be thought of as being in central Europe, as it is equidistant between the continent's easternmost and westernmost points, the Ural Mountains and the Atlantic Ocean. It's also halfway between the North Pole and the Equator. At 91,699 square miles (237,500 sq. km), it is the fourth-largest country in central and eastern Europe. It is bordered by Bulgaria to the south, Serbia to the southwest, Hungary to the northwest, and Ukraine and the Republic of Moldova to the north and northeast. The eastern coast meets the Black Sea. The Danube River runs along the southern border with Bulgaria for just under 670 miles (1,075 km) before turning north and reaching the Black Sea as the Danube Delta. The capital, Bucharest, is between 250 and 700 miles (400 to 1,100 km)

Decebal Head sculpture, along the banks of the Danube Gorges.

from such other major cities as Belgrade, Istanbul, Sofia, Budapest, and Vienna.

Romania's terrain is evenly split between mountains, hills, and plains. The countryside reflects a rather ad hoc form of agriculture; orchards and vineyards are often charmingly disorderly. There are lushly green areas flecked with haystacks, bright yellow sunflower fields, and dense forests. The mountains can be snowcapped or verdant depending on the season, not unlike those of Switzerland or Austria. The highest point is Moldoveanu Peak, at 8,346 feet (2,544 meters), in the Southern Carpathians. Natural resources include oil, natural gas, coal, iron ore, nonferrous ore (primarily copper, lead, and zinc), gold and silver, sulfur, timber, and salt.

One of the country's most interesting geographical areas is the Danube Delta (Delta Dunării), Europe's largest and best-preserved delta. A UNESCO World Heritage Site, it is home to three hundred species of birds, twelve hundred kinds of plants, and forty-five species of freshwater fish.

CLIMATE AND WEATHER

Romania's position on the edge of the continental landmass gives it elements of both temperate and continental weather. It is also somewhat protected by the Carpathian mountain range, which serves as a barrier to both Atlantic air masses and Russian climatic influences. The climate can certainly be on the extreme side, however; Bucharest summers can see the temperature soar to over 104°F (40°C), while rural winter lows can be as harsh as 14°F (-10°C) or worse, with summers averaging at about 72°F (23°C) and winters 27°F (-3°C). The two main seasons are long, and seem to be encroaching more and more on spring and fall. Indeed, November, December, and even January can have temperate days in the Fahrenheit fifties (Celsius mid-teens). Seasons can change quite abruptly, although spring and fall can have long periods of very pleasant weather.

In the south, the average annual temperature is 51.8° F (11°C); in the north it's slightly lower at 46.4°F

(8°C). Perhaps the best weather is in the southeast of the country, where Mediterranean influences bring mild, warm conditions. Rain is usually not a problem outside the mountain areas—although when it does come, it often comes with a vengeance, and the country's substandard drainage systems can be overwhelmed. In the cities this seldom results in anything worse than wet socks, but some parts of rural Romania are severely affected by floods every few years, often with a few deaths. Snowfall in winter can also be severe.

A BRIEF HISTORY

Romanians put a lot of their contemporary woes down to historical causes, and with good reason. A relatively powerless country—which, its citizens are proud to tell you, has never invaded another state—Romania's location has left it at the mercy of great, and often aggressive, neighboring foreign empires. It has been rarely left in peace long enough to develop a sense of its own identity. The Communist era, as we will see, had the biggest effect, leaving a legacy of bureaucracy, mutual suspicion, and corruption, along with an awe for most things Western.

Prehistory to Post-Romans

The first traces of human habitation in what is now Romania date back to the Stone Age. Around 10,000 years ago, settled communities relied on hunting, farming, and breeding stock. Estimates vary as to when the Thracians, a group of Indo-European tribes, arrived from the south, but by around 500 BCE they had mixed with the local people to form the Dacians. The Dacians, in turn, split into various tribes, federations, and kingdoms; and under their greatest king, Burebista, who ruled in the first century BCE, they became so powerful that the Romans began to take heed. Julius Caesar decided to wage war against the Dacians but was assassinated before he had the chance—shortly before Burebista met the same fate, slain by his own noblemen. The state was subsequently split into four pieces, then reunified.

Meanwhile, the Roman Empire was growing in might and territory, and the Roman emperor Trajan eventually conquered Dacia in 106 CE. The Romans held on for over a century and a half until successive incursions from the Barbarians prompted them to withdraw, but their brief period of rule was a significant one for the country; they brought a unified Latin language and Christianity, as well as advances in farming, mining, commerce, arts, crafts, and culture.

The years immediately following Roman rule saw the future Romania governed in succession by the Gothic, Hunnish, Avar, and First Bulgarian empires. Throughout this chopping and changing, the Daco-Romans did their best to continue life in their villages. Their language was developing, as was their religion, under the guidance of the Orthodox Byzantine Empire at Constantinople.

The Middle Ages and Some Famous Names

By the tenth century the region was divided into small zones, and these eventually merged into three feudal states or principalities—Transylvania, Moldavia, and Wallachia. These are still recognized today, albeit no longer with any administrative relevance. The Magyars of Hungary conquered Transylvania in the eleventh century, an act that still has ramifications in the present day. It was at this time that the Székely (a Hungarian-speaking ethnic group), the Teutonic Order, and the Saxons were invited by their Hungarian kings to settle in Transylvania. From 1453, however, Moldavia and Wallachia had a new fight on their hands when the Ottoman Turks conquered Constantinople. While the Ottomans expanded their empire through the annexation of much of Hungary and the Balkans, the Romanian principalities held out, with their princes heading the Christian resistance for several hundred years.

Most legendary among these princes—for very different reasons—were Stephen the Great and Vlad the Impaler (Vlad Țepeș in Romanian). The latter ruled Wallachia three times: in 1448, from 1456 to 1462, and again in 1476. His notoriety stems from the cruel tortures he inflicted on a variety of victims, from local peasants to invading Ottomans, the most infamous being death by impalement. A local legend suggests that under Țepeș, it was possible to leave a bag of gold in the street, where it would remain untouched, so great was the fear of punishment. There were also rumors—which historians do not credit—of cannibalism, which led to Țepeș' inclusion in the Dracula mythos. Despite his sadism, however, in Romania Țepeș is remembered chiefly for his justice and spirited defense against the Ottomans, whom he successfully held at bay for some time.

Vlad the Impaler's contemporary, Stephen III of Moldavia, or Stephen the Great (Ștefan cel Mare), is remembered for different reasons. Throughout his long reign (1457–1504), he fortified Moldavia, preserved his

Sixteenth century portrait of Vlad III, known as Vlad the Impaler.

state from Hungarian, Polish, and Ottoman attempts to conquer it, and won thirty-four out of thirty-six battles he waged. One of these was a historical first, a Christian victory over the Ottomans that led Pope Sixtus IV to pronounce him *verus christianae fidei athleta*, or "True Champion of Christian Faith." Aside from the cultural development that took place during his reign, his legacy includes the many churches and monasteries that today are UNESCO World Heritage Sites.

Despite the efforts of Vlad the Impaler and Stephen the Great, though, the Romanian principalities could not hold the Ottomans at bay indefinitely without help from the West, and were obliged to recognize Turkish suzerainty. They were never occupied, however, and unlike much of the rest of the area, never became provinces or had Turkish governors, instead paying a tribute to the Turks for the privilege of retaining their autonomy. At this time the Romanian states were the protectors of Christianity for the entire Orthodox East.

The Beginnings of Modern Romania

The defeat of the Ottomans did not put an end to foreign intervention in Romania. In 1699 the Treaty of Karlowitz gave Transylvania to Habsburg Austria. The Austrians in turn co-opted Oltenia, part of Wallachia, in 1718, and held on to it for almost two decades. This was followed by the Habsburg seizure of Bucovina in northwest Moldavia in 1775. The Russians also got in on the game by occupying Basarabia, the eastern half of Moldavia, in

An illustration of Wallachia from fifteenth century biblical encyclopedia The Nuremberg Chronicle.

1812. Indeed, the period was marked by the growing political influence of the Russian Empire, a power that would come to dominate the Romanian political landscape until the late twentieth century.

Meanwhile, the late eighteenth century had seen the emergence of a Romanian bourgeoisie whose sense of shared identity prompted calls for the union of the three states into an independent country. The wave of liberal revolutions that swept through Europe in 1848 reached Romania with popular democratic uprisings in the three principalities. The first phase of the union—the merging of Moldavia and Wallachia—was achieved in 1859, after Russia's defeat in the Crimean War. At the time, the new entity was ruled by the elected Prince Alexandru Ioan Cuza, but seven years later a combination of scandal and political opposition forced him to abdicate, and he was succeeded by the German Prince Carol (Karl) I of the house of Hohenzollern-Sigmaringen.

Trouble with the Turks simmered on. In 1877–78, Romania fought with Russia against the Ottomans. Its contribution was considered instrumental, and the country was recognized as an independent state in the 1878 Treaty of Berlin, making it the first independent national state in Eastern Europe. It became a kingdom three years later, with Carol I as its first king. This did not address the issue of Transylvania, however, which by then had become part of Hungary, despite the protestations of the 70 percent of its inhabitants who were Romanian. The period also saw early emigration from Romania to the US and Canada, in search of economic opportunities and freedom from political oppression.

The World Wars

Surrounded by three huge empires, Romania turned westward for guidance in its cultural, educational, military, and administrative development. It cultivated a particular affinity with France, eventually joining the Western Allies during the First World War in 1916 and declaring war on Austro-Hungary. Its aim was to win back Transylvania, which was accomplished at the end of the war, along with the inclusion of various minorities living in the region. Its campaign, however, was less than illustrious. Two-thirds of the country, including Bucharest, were occupied by the Central Powers, and in 1918 it was obliged to negotiate a peace treaty with Germany, although it did rejoin the war five months later.

By the end of the war, the country had almost doubled its size and population. Greater Romania (România Mare) saw the different regions officially united, a period still fondly remembered; a modern-day political party even uses the phrase as its name to recall the pride of that era. Some of the country's most beautiful buildings, typically designed by foreign architects, date from this time, earning Bucharest the appellation "the Paris of the East."

For two decades after the end of the war, the country was a liberal constitutional monarchy, bringing economic and cultural advances, a relatively functional democracy, and some press freedom, but tension was developing around its minorities. Twenty-eight percent of the Romanian population was made up of Magyars (ethnic Hungarians), Germans, Jews, Ukrainians, and Bulgarians, among others. These people sought representation, and several political parties giving voice to them sprang up. Unfortunately, nationalistic and anti-Semitic parties were also gaining in popularity. One, the Iron Guard, won 15.5 percent of the vote in the 1937 general elections.

Carol II, having renounced the throne in 1925, returned from exile in Paris in 1930 to supplant his son Mihai (Michael) as king. He soon began to feel the rising pressure of fascism, and the following year joined many countries in continental Europe by establishing a dictatorship. With public disenchantment with the political parties running high, and violence commonly used to end political arguments, there was little opposition to Carol's decision to abolish Parliament. Already scandalizing even the most ardent royalists with his licentious private life, he banned all other political parties and began to rule the country with help from a disreputable coterie of personal advisers, many of whom were introduced to him by his mistress Elena Lupescu.

Unsurprisingly, things did not go well. In 1940 Romania lost territory to the USSR (through occupation) and Hungary (through the Vienna Dictate) without a shot being fired. Carol II was forced to abdicate in favor of his son, Mihai, but power was effectively taken over by General Ion Antonescu with the help of the Iron Guard, which he later suppressed. Antonescu became a military dictator, leaving Mihai king in name alone. In 1941 Romania entered the Second World War under the command of the German Wehrmacht in order to get back its territories from the Allies, and was awarded Transnistria by the Nazis.

King Mihai (Michael) I, 1947.

In 1944 a pro-Allies coup by King Mihai resulted in the arrest of Antonescu and the placing of Romanian forces under Red Army control, after which they sustained heavy losses fighting the Nazis in Hungary and Czechoslovakia. After the war, the Paris Peace Treaty saw northern Transylvania (which had been annexed by Hungary) returned to Romania; but the northern

THE HOLOCAUST IN ROMANIA

Anti-Semitism, which had grown worldwide in the nineteenth century, played a big part in public and political discourse in the interwar period with the rise of right-wing, nationalistic parties. Jews were barred from professional associations, forbidden to marry Christians, and forced in some cases to reapply for citizenship. In Romania, eighty anti-Jewish laws were passed in two years at the start of the 1940s, and the Iron Guard began a campaign of violence and looting against Jews. In 1941, in one incident alone, over 13,000 Jews were killed in the Iaşi pogrom.

The persecution continued after the fall of the Iron Guard, when the Antonescu regime allied itself with Nazi Germany. Deportations stopped in 1943, when Antonescu began to seek peace with the Allies, but oppression of the country's Jewish citizens continued.

It was not until 2003 that Romania set up the Wiesel Commission to investigate and educate the public about the country's role in the Holocaust. Its report assessed that between 280,000 and 380,000 Romanian Jews were killed. The commission was set up in response to international outcry after top Romanian politicians, including President Iliescu, denied that Romania had participated in the Holocaust. Only recently has it begun being studied and commemorated in the country.

territory lost to the USSR was never recovered, and went on to become the modern Republic of Moldova. The 1945 Yalta Agreement saw Romania, along with the rest of Eastern Europe, allotted to the Soviet "sphere of influence," marking the start of Romania's shift to Communism.

Communism

The Russian occupation of Romania at the end of the Second World War saw the abdication and exile of King Mihai, and the establishment of a Communist People's Republic in 1947. Soviet economic methods were adopted, farming was collectivized, properties were seized by the state, and traditional Romanian culture was altered or obliterated. The country's first Communist leader was former tramway worker Gheorghe Gheorghiu-Dej. Initially an ardent Stalinist—his anti-Semitic campaign coincided with Stalin's own Jewish purges—he also toed the line of Stalin's successor, Nikita Khrushchev. Khrushchev advocated peaceful coexistence with the West, and subsequently withdrew Soviet troops from Romania. When Gheorghiu-Dej became the president of the country in 1961, however, he turned his back on Soviet policy, a stance that won him favor in the West, and began a campaign of industrialization. Before he died in 1965, he also opened diplomatic relations with the West, including the US.

Following Gheorghiu-Dej's death, the helm of the country passed to Nicolae Ceaușescu, a former shoemaker's apprentice and hitherto low-profile figure who had joined the Communist Party in the early 1930s, when it was still an illegal organization. During a jail term in 1943 for his antifascist activities, Ceaușescu had shared a cell with Gheorghiu-Dej; he went on to become his protégé, rising steadily up the party rankings. He continued his predecessor's assertion of Romanian independence from Soviet influence, denouncing Russia's invasion of Czechoslovakia in 1968. This won him fans among both his people and Western leaders; he was awarded the Danish Order of the Elephant and was made an honorary Knight Grand Cross of the Order of the Bath, a British order of chivalry, although both were later rescinded. Life in Romania was less repressive in the early days of Ceaușescu's rule, although the Securitate, the country's brutal secret police, were fully functioning. Contraception and abortion were banned, and the childless were heavily taxed to encourage population growth.

Ceaușescu's Personality Cult

It was following Ceaușescu's visit to China, North Korea, and Vietnam in 1971 that the political situation in Romania worsened considerably. Ceaușescu was tremendously impressed with the hardline version of Communism he saw in Asia, and upon his return he set about replicating it at home. He expanded the power and reach of the party, and increased censorship, propaganda, and the indoctrination of young people. He also began to build up a personality cult, indulging himself—and his wife, Elena, who played an increasingly important role—with grand public pageants. As his lifestyle grew ever more lavish, the Romanian people were sinking into miserable deprivation. The initial economic growth built on the back of foreign loans had turned to grinding poverty. Long lines for scarce meat, bread, and fruit were commonplace, and food was rationed, as were electricity, heating, and gas. Although the Gheorghiu-Dej policy of industrialization had been kept, little of what was produced was of high enough quality to be sold abroad. Meanwhile, the Securitate had practically made Romania a police state.

"Systematization," the disastrous mass rehousing policy introduced in 1974, saw large areas razed and rural people resettled in cities. Churches, monasteries, and homes were demolished wholesale to make way for poorly funded "prestige" projects that often did not reach completion. The monotonous, substandard apartment complexes that were erected as part of the systematization drive still scar Romania's cities and towns. The centerpiece of the policy was the Palace of the People (*Casa Poporului*), a giant administrative building that remains one of the biggest in the world (as well as the official heaviest in the world, at 9 billion pounds). Work began in 1984 and, although the building is in use, it is still not finished.

By 1989, Communist regimes were falling across Eastern Europe, leaving Ceaușescu increasingly isolated. Prompted by government attempts to evict a Hungarian clergyman who had criticized the regime in the international press, a protest broke out in the western city of Timișoara among the pastor's parishioners. They

Nicolae Ceaușescu, 1965.

were soon joined by passersby, many of whom were students who believed the eviction was another attempt to restrict religious freedom. Over the following days the protest grew and intensified. The army was sent in, and dozens of protesters were shot. The government dispatched workers from the neighboring region of Oltenia to suppress the demonstrations, but instead they joined the protesters.

On December 21, the state organized a mass rally in Bucharest to condemn the Timișoara uprising. Ceaușescu was in the middle of a speech from the balcony of the Central Committee building when bangs were heard, which were later attributed to the Securitate firing on the crowd. The people, initially afraid, started to jeer at the Communist leader; after attempts to quell the dissent failed, Ceaușescu and his wife fled inside the building, then attempted to escape by helicopter. Meanwhile, the Bucharest protesters began to riot.

Government forces fired on the people. Hundreds died from bullets and stab wounds, or were crushed by tanks. Fire trucks turned their water jets on the public, while the police beat and arrested people. Eventually, and for unclear reasons, the security forces switched sides to fight alongside the demonstrators. In all, more than a thousand people died in the week of protests. The Ceaușescus were arrested by the army, put on "trial" for genocide against their own people by a self-designated extraordinary military tribunal, and shot on Christmas Day. Many of the details surrounding the revolution still remain unclear, and rumors of foreign instigation persist.

After Communism

The joy that followed the fall of the Ceaușescus was short-lived. Rather than power going to someone untainted by the old regime, the figure who emerged as the new leader was Ion Iliescu, a Communist Party official who had been seen as a threat and sidelined by Ceaușescu. Even before the old leader was shot, he had seized control of the country with other party members as the leader of the new National Salvation Front (FSN), which became the provisional ruling authority. The sudden converts to democracy repealed some of the most unpopular Communist laws and ran as candidates in the May 1990 elections, where—thanks to the FSN's stranglehold on the media—they were overwhelming winners. The new government was packed with former Communist officials, who tried to persist with a socialist agenda.

Horrified by the direction their new "democracy" was taking, Bucharest protesters again took to the streets. Iliescu denounced the demonstrators, led by university students and professors, as "hooligans," and called in miners to quash the protests. In the infamous "Mineriad" of June 1990, the workers set about clubbing the protesters, killing more than a hundred people, according to NGO estimates, and wounding another thousand. Iliescu later thanked the miners for stopping "the fascist attempt to create a *coup d'état*." A year later the miners were back in the capital, calling for higher wages, and this is eventually what finally brought down the government.

Throughout the 1990s, Romania struggled to shake off its Communist legacy. The economy shrank and inflation was rampant, sometimes higher than 300 percent. Poverty was, if anything, initially worse. Things did not start to improve until the former Communists lost power in the general elections of 1996, following the start of media liberalization and a better organized opposition. Major reforms were then implemented. Iliescu managed to hang on to the presidency, twice winning reelection, and remained on the scene until as late as 2004. His prime minister was Adrian Nastase, who was repeatedly accused of wrongdoing, including corruption, bribery, money laundering, trafficking influence, and censorship. He was eventually jailed in 2012 and again in 2014, a development that would have been unthinkable only a few years beforehand, and which was hailed as a major success in the fight against corruption.

Looking West

The year 2004 promised to herald a new era for Romania.

Iliescu departed from politics, barred by the constitution from seeking a third term (it was decided that his first tenure did not count toward the total of two). In a vote that attracted the usual accusations of electoral fraud, Nastase (campaigning through the Social Democrat Party [PSD]) was defeated by the charismatic mayor of Bucharest, Traian Basescu, a former ship's captain. On top of that, Romania was accepted into NATO.

Three years later, on January 1, 2007, came EU accession. This was a great boost to the country's economy and self-image, and saw foreign investment flood into the country—although the lifting of travel and eventually work restrictions saw high numbers of citizens also flood out. The economic boom was brought to an abrupt end by the global financial crisis—stunning many young Romanians, who had known nothing but expansion—as the property bubble burst, along with widespread job losses, bankruptcies, and austerity measures. However, by 2013 GDP growth was back in healthy territory.

Throughout this period of flux, Basescu remained in power until 2014, despite various clashes with his prime ministerial appointees. The most acrimonious of these was with the PSD's youthful Victor Ponta, who sought to succeed Basescu after the latter's second and final term as president. The 2014 election was hugely controversial. What were widely condemned as flagrant and deliberate efforts by Ponta and his party to prevent Romania's sizeable diaspora from voting (younger and more educated than the national average, those emigrants typically disdained the PSD) led to huge lines forming outside Romanian embassies abroad and public outrage back home. The ploy was in vain, however: Ponta lost to Klaus Iohannis, the ethnic German former mayor of Sibiu, who campaigned on an anti-corruption platform. The triumph of "the good guy," combined with economic recovery and a wider clampdown on graft, reignited some of the pre-crisis hope that living standards would continue to rise and the country would finally shake off its Communist legacy.

Iohannis was returned to power in 2019, where he remained until the controversial 2024/25 presidential election, prevented by the constitution from running again. But the period was not plain sailing for Romania. The undeniable gains of the country opening up were not distributed evenly throughout the population: while educated young English-speaking urbanites earned Western-level monthly salaries, the older generation who came of age under Communism, particularly rural dwellers, felt left behind by the country's progress. Many elderly and even some middle-aged Romanians hark back to the "good old days of Ceaușescu when everyone had a job." While this may be largely attributable to the universal tendency to view the days of one's youth through rose-tinted glasses, the impact of their grievances—what they view as EU favoring of richer members than them, and the encroachment of "Western propaganda" such as support for LGBTQ rights—has threatened to impede Romania's ongoing metaphorical drift Westwards. It is essentially a replication of political patterns also seen elsewhere, such as Brexit in the UK, or the rise of Donald Trump in the US. (The slogan "make Romania great again" has recently begun rearing its head.)

Indeed, in the 2024 presidential election, out of nowhere a charismatic, far-right demagogue named Călin Georgescu rode the wave of a viral TikTok campaign largely believed to be funded by Russia to triumph in the first round. His implausible declaration of zero campaign funding led to the vote being annulled on grounds of "interference by a foreign actor." This shocking and unprecedented move split public opinion: while some praised the authorities for having the courage to thwart what was widely considered a Russian coup, others felt outraged that their vote had counted for nothing. Whichever side they came down on, most felt that the joy of their post-Communist freedom had been tainted, leaving Romanian democracy rather battered and bruised, although the ultimate election the next year of Europhile Nicușor Dan reaffirmed that the country sees its future best served with closer EU integration.

President Nicușor Dan.

The Romanian Palace of the Parliament, Bucharest.

GOVERNMENT

Romania's constitution dates from 1991, although it was amended in 2003. The document establishes the country as a democracy and market economy, and enshrines the values of human dignity, civic rights and freedoms, the unhindered development of the individual, justice, and political pluralism. It obliges the state to implement free trade, protect competition, and provide a favorable framework for production. It also establishes the structure of the government, providing for a president, a parliament, a constitutional court, and a separate system of civil and criminal courts, including a supreme court.

A democratic republic, Romania's system of government is semi-presidential—president and prime minister share executive functions, and both participate in day-to-day state administration. The president, who is the head of state, is voted in by the public, and their official residence is Cotroceni Palace in Bucharest. The presidential tenure was increased from four to five years by constitutional amendment in 2003, and the president can hold office for up to two terms. Their duties include safeguarding the constitution, overseeing foreign affairs, and ensuring the proper functioning of public authorities. They are also supreme commander of the armed forces and chairman of the Supreme Defense Council, and can mediate between state powers as well as between the government and the public.

The prime minister, based at Victoria Palace, Bucharest, is the head of government and picks the members of their cabinet, which is subject to a parliamentary vote of approval. Typically the prime minister is the head of the ruling party or coalition; but if no party has a majority, they are appointed by the president.

Parliament is bicameral, with a Senate (*Senat*) of 134 members and a Chamber of Deputies (*Camera Deputaților*) with 331. Both chambers hold elections every four years. Elected officials are selected on the basis of party lists through proportional representation, with the exception of the president and mayors. The voting age is eighteen, and there is universal suffrage.

The country is divided into forty-one administrative counties (*judeti*), plus the capital, Bucharest, each of which is run by an elected county council and mayor. A prefect is appointed in each by the government, who is responsible for public services and central agencies at the local level. The prefect can block a local authority action if they consider it illegal or unconstitutional; the matter is then referred to an administrative court. Local councils are responsible for spending the budgets they receive from the state.

POLITICS

Romania's turbulent post-Communist political landscape has seen some significant changes in its party lineup. Traditionally, the main two parties have been the center-left PSD (the Social Democratic Party), formed by Communist Party members following the revolution; and the PNL (National Liberal Party), a centrist party whose leader, Klaus Iohannis, served as president from 2014 to 2025. Several smaller parties have seen their influence wax and wane; the Democratic Union of Hungarians in Romania (UDMR), an alliance that represents ethnic Hungarians, has had more staying power than most.

However, the 2024/25 presidential election saw the political battlefield redrawn, with the liberal-leaning progressive centrists going head to head with the nationalist far right. The "first" first round, in 2024, saw Elena Lasconi, head of the center-right Save Romania Union (USR), come a narrow second to Călin Georgescu, a Covid-denying far-right conspiracy theorist, whose dizzying political ascent from nowhere via a viral TikTok campaign with zero declared financing provoked suspicions of Russian interference, leading to the controversial and unprecedented annulment of the vote and his ultimate disqualification from the rerun ballot. Said rerun saw USR-supported independent Bucharest mayor Nicuşor Dan, a Sorbonne-educated staunchly Europhile mathematician, overturn the commanding lead of George Simion, head of the far-right Alliance for the Union of Romanians (AUR) and described by *The Economist* as a "MAGA-based rabble-rouser." It was widely viewed as Romania affirming its Westward leanings and rejecting Russian influence.

Personalities have long overshadowed policies and principles in Romanian politics. Expedient alliances are regularly forged across supposed ideological divides, and the loss of a strong figurehead can see an organization wither. Perhaps this focus on people over policies explains why Romanian politics is characterized by highly personal attacks. In the run-up to elections, prominent public figures are widely accused of many things, including homosexuality, rape, corruption, and collaboration with the Securitate. Elections also routinely come with allegations of fraud, voter suppression, censorship, and organized multiple voting, and Parliament is regularly voted among the least trusted institutions in Romanian public life.

THE ECONOMY

The Romanian economy has been through something of a roller-coaster ride since the collapse of Communism. In

1989 it was in a dire state, with an obsolete industrial base, and it continued to decline until 1993. A major problem was repayment of debt to the West. Ceaușescu had run up huge arrears in building up state-owned industry in the 1970s. Determined to be free of foreign creditors, he ordered all efforts to go into repaying the debts, leaving his own people with little to sustain them and the economy in tatters. Things got worse before they got better, with the economy shrinking through much of the 1990s. The government implemented an ambitious program of structural reforms in the areas of energy-intensive industries, agriculture, the financial sector, and macroeconomic stabilization.

Industrial manufacturing and services contribute the greatest share to the Romanian economy. The main industries are agriculture, banking and finance, defense, IT, manufacturing, healthcare, and renewable energy. According to the United Nations' Human Development Indicators for 2020, skilled employees make up 81.7 percent of the national labor force. Around 1.8 million people, or 21 percent of the total workforce, are employed in agriculture, a declining share; the manufacturing sector accounts for the largest slice.

One rapidly growing area is IT. A combination of well-trained programmers, tax breaks, and relatively low labor costs have seen the software sector mushroom over the past couple of decades, and Romanian techies enjoy an enviable reputation abroad. The industry outpaced the overall economy nearly threefold over 2015–2020. (The unfortunate underbelly of all this online savvy is an equally buoyant criminal community: the small town of Râmnicu Vâlcea, for example, has been dubbed the global capital of cybercrime.)

Unemployment is persistently lower than the EU average, notwithstanding some increases with the global financial crisis and the pandemic. In 2025 it stood at below 6 percent.

STUCK IN THE MIDDLE

Romanians tend to blame many of their historical and current woes on their country's location. Wedged between the Russian, Ottoman, and Austro-Hungarian empires, the country was subject to repeated invasions and buffeted between various foreign powers. Many believe that, given this history, no country could have emerged unscathed. Some Romanians feel bitter that their country was delivered into the Soviet sphere of influence at the end of the Second World War, and think that if it had been located further west on the map, things would have been much better.

Influences from both East and West are evident in today's Romania. Many of the country's young people are very Westernized. They learn English and other Western European languages with enthusiasm and dedication, consume largely Western (particularly American) media in the form of music, films, and online content, dress like their European peers, and long for their country to continue its assimilation and appropriation of EU standards. On the other hand, some Romanians (mainly older) hark back to the Soviet era and its values. They bemoan the licentiousness that they perceive as a Western disease, which they see in LGBTQ and trans rights, the increasing legalization of drugs, and sexual freedom. A subgroup, the Roma community, retains Eastern influences. Some Roma women dress in traditional Indian-style costumes, while the men favor Syrian- and Turkish-influenced suits and shoes with pointed toes—although the majority attire themselves like the rest of the population.

A PERIOD OF TRANSITION

It is difficult for an outsider to understand how bad life was in Romania even just four decades ago. Emerging from this dark period, and with EU membership giving an added impetus to reform, the country has been changing at breakneck speed. The pace of this change is visible in the cityscapes, which often seem to resemble a metropolitan-sized construction site. Businesses spring up and close down frequently. Fluctuating currency exchange rates and macroeconomic indicators have been unpredictable. And once the country seemed to have finally entered a period of post-crisis relative stability, the pandemic added another abrupt reversal.

The transition period has also had a notable effect on the country's value system. After nearly half a century of censorship, Romania was suddenly exposed to news, views, and—perhaps most obviously—products and commercialism from the outside world. Romanians were suddenly forced to question much of what they had believed in for decades. This is perhaps one reason why some unfounded opinions remain (especially about the West), as well as strong belief among some in superstitions. Other effects of the sudden arrival of capitalism include a general susceptibility to big business and advertising; having had no exposure to commercials, Romanians had not developed the savvy of the Western consumer, although people have become a little more skeptical since the 2008 Global Financial Crisis. Meanwhile, the sudden acquisition of wealth led to the formation of a Romanian *nouveau riche*, a moneyed class trying to behave like an elite.

BUCHAREST

The provenance of the name Bucharest is uncertain, but one suggestion is that the settlement was founded by a shepherd called Bucur. Burned down by the Ottomans and abandoned by the Romanian princes in the early seventeenth century, Bucharest was rebuilt and prospered, despite being afflicted over the next two hundred years by a plague, a devastating fire, and various occupations. Officially chosen as the capital in 1881 when the Kingdom of Romania was established, Bucharest's population grew rapidly, while cultural and architectural advances earned it the moniker "Little Paris."

During the Second World War, Bucharest suffered bombardment by both the Allies and the Axis powers, due to shifting alliances (which we'll explore more in a bit). The Communist government that was established at the end of the war changed the face of the city, with grim, monotonous apartment blocks built as part of the process of systematization, and large parts of the old town razed to make way for the civic center and the grandiose People's Palace. A massive earthquake in 1977, measuring 7.4 on the Richter Scale, also brought down many old buildings. The city continues to be subject to upheaval, now in the form of the many urban regeneration projects intended to bring its housing, facilities, and infrastructure up to twenty-first-century Western standards. It is now brightened by designer boutiques and capitalist trappings that would have made its Communist rulers wince.

Today Bucharest is by far the most important city in the country in terms of size and economics. With a population of about 1.7 million, it is the seventh-largest capital in the European Union, bisected by the Dâmbovița River. The city does not have as many instantly recognizable landmarks as some other capitals. Its most distinctive edifice is the former People's Palace, now officially known as Parliament Palace (*Palatul Parlamentului*). While there is some pride that the country has (nearly) completed such a big construction project, most Bucharest inhabitants prefer the

The Unirii area of Bucharest.

Athenaeum, a neoclassical concert hall in the center of the city. The Athenaeum is no more than a few hundred meters from the former Central Committee building, from where Ceaușescu delivered his final address, which is now part of the Senate.

THE COUNTRYSIDE

In order to understand the "real Romania," one should head for the countryside. While residents of the main cities enjoy rising wages, increasing prosperity, and decent shops and restaurants, the rural areas show how far Romania still has to go. Although close to half the population lives in the countryside, these areas are still poorly supplied with essential goods and services. While the situation has improved significantly, helped by EU funds, some people still live without running water, relying on outside

The village Hosman, near Sibiu in Transylvania.

latrines and wells. The horse and cart is a regular sight on rural roads. Some villages are without a doctor, there are few banks, and shops often have an only basic range of goods. Subsistence farming supports many families, unemployment is higher, and salaries are lower. Connectivity rates are also lower (although the gap is narrowing). It should also be noted that a mountain village in a popular tourist area represents a different slice of rural life than a village in the poorer northeastern region.

Despite these disadvantages, the Romanian countryside is in some respects the backbone of the national culture. Costume, cuisine, and folk music all developed from rural traditions. Because of migration to the cities—both voluntary for economic reasons and the forced displacement that took place under Communism—a large percentage of the urban population are either from the countryside or are the children of rural people, and some pastoral customs continue to be observed in towns.

CHAPTER **TWO**

VALUES & ATTITUDES

At first sight, particularly in the cities, Romania might seem to differ little from other Western democracies. People spend time with family and friends, are notionally if not devoutly religious, and enjoy shopping, sports, and socializing. Further interaction with locals, however, reveals significant quirks in the Romanian psyche. Many of today's city dwellers have parents and grandparents from the country, and rural religions, ideas, and customs dominate the culture. This is particularly evident in the superstitions to which many people cling. The result is that despite the provocative dress of some Romanian women—even professional ones—and suggestive images on billboards, attitudes toward sexual matters remain largely traditional.

The other big influence is, of course—even if the Romanians are fed up of hearing it said—Communism. To cover the many ways in which the old regime has left its mark on modern-day mores would require a whole book itself. A suspicion born of years of living among secret

Securitate informers, the suppression of civic spirit (though this has revivified in recent years), and a weary acceptance of everyday difficulties are among the main consequences, along with a deference to authority figures. The deep-seated Communist legacy is at odds with young Romanians' eager embrace of all things Western, creating the tension that characterizes this society in transition. Despite all the social upheaval, though, some things, such as the warm Romanian hospitality, have remained constant.

ORPHANS, DOGS, AND DRACULA

Romanians have a keen awareness of the stereotyping that they are convinced clouds all foreigners' perceptions of them, especially when it comes to orphans, stray dogs, and Dracula. Although Romanian child care has progressed significantly since haunting images of malnourished children in institutions were broadcast across the Western world in the early 1990s, the subsequent lack of media interest in reporting improvements means that many foreigners retain the association. Stray dogs were indeed once a serious problem, but following a cull and efforts to encourage the adoption of strays, far fewer ownerless canines roam the streets today. The Dracula associations, meanwhile, can be traced back to Irish writer Bram Stoker's incorporation of Vlad Țepeș and his Transylvanian setting into his 1897 novel. Few Romanians had even heard of the Dracula myth before the end of Communist rule in 1989, and were initially bemused when tourists began arriving in Transylvania, expecting a countryside dotted with sinister Gothic castles. (Bran Castle near Brașov, which has become a sort of unofficial Dracula's castle, simply because of Țepeș having reportedly spent a couple of days in its dungeon, is in fact a rather pretty building, offering little in the way of macabre thrills.)

Since EU accession, however, which now permits Romanians to travel visa-free throughout the bloc, another and more controversial stereotype has caused much more disquiet: the conflation of Romanians with the Roma, and the latter's reputation for criminality in Western Europe. Many Romanians feel aggrieved that what they see as the Roma's propensity for pickpocketing, begging, prostitution, and suchlike has tarnished their nationality's image, reflecting unfavorably on their compatriots who have headed west for honest toil.

PATRIOTISM AND ANTI-PATRIOTISM

Romanians generally divide into two camps: the fervently patriotic and the terminally cynical. Anyone who grew up under the Communist regime was repeatedly told how wonderful their country was, and that they were lucky to be experiencing a "golden age" (poverty and deprivation notwithstanding). There was no source of objective news from the outside world, and rumors that the Western world was decadent, crime-stricken, and drug-ravaged gained currency. Although information about the world is now available to anyone who is inclined to look for it, comforting ideas about the greatness of Romania have been harder to budge, particularly among the older generation. Some still hark back to the Communist era as a golden one, citing the former high levels of employment, low crime rate, and lack of drugs to back up their case.

In the other corner is the cynical younger generation. They are typically fluent in English (among other languages), and keen students of life outside their borders. Sickened by the corruption and deprivation that have hindered progress, some tend to assume the worst of their homeland, and often react to the latest political or business scandal with a sardonic shrug; such individuals have also taken a prominent role in some of the street protests (against corruption and for EU integration) of recent years. Typically well educated, many are keen to travel abroad and sometimes feel embarrassed to be identified as Romanian, believing this leads foreigners to make certain negative assumptions about them. They have a wry motto about their homeland: "Romania's a nice country—shame it's populated."

Whether they esteem their country highly or not, though, the majority of Romanians care about what happens to it. Those who leave tend to do so as a last resort; many young, educated people feel a responsibility to stay and use their skills and values to make things better. This is usually the option favored over going abroad, and many who do emigrate fully intend to return after making enough money to secure themselves a decent life here. This view is seldom presented in the tabloids of Western Europe, which assumes that people from Romania are desperate to get out and settle in the West permanently. Some are and do, but many others see their stay abroad as a short sojourn to improve their economic circumstances before returning to a better life back home.

THE LATIN TEMPERAMENT

Romania is a Latin country culturally. People are typically demonstrative, talking loudly and emphasizing their points with dramatic gestures. Many are quickly moved to emotion, which is conveyed through raising both the volume and the pitch of the voice—it's not uncommon for men to end up exchanging squeaks if they get into an argument. To an outsider, many straightforward discussions between Romanians appear to be altercations, because they are delivered with what seems like fury. If a Romanian addresses you in a blunt or animated way, do not assume they are angry with you—it is more likely that this is their normal demeanor. Conversations come with frequent interruptions, and if two people are talking at the same time, there is no guarantee that one will feel obliged to stop. Don't feel offended when people interrupt, as they are not being deliberately rude—in the flurry that is a Romanian conversation, sometimes interrupting is the only way to be heard.

This said, the hot Latin temper is also in evidence. Romanians can be quickly moved to anger, although often this is about not losing face rather than a serious intent to follow through; it is rare to see arguments actually coming to blows. In terms of public behavior, many Romanians are uninhibited. There is no embargo on public displays of affection, and amorous couples can assume quite intimate positions in public, particularly in parks, with no sense of impropriety. The Latin *joie de vivre* also comes out when people let their hair down. Nightclubs and parties are usually vibrant affairs, often going on late into the night. Rarely will you see a miserable Romanian in a club, complaining about the DJ.

Owing to shortages and periods of social upheaval, Romanians have not been able to develop the famous style and elegance associated with other Latin countries in Europe, such as the Italians—with whom they most closely identify—and the French. They do exhibit proclivities in this direction, however, and many spend a lot of time, money, and effort on their physical appearance. Some people are also fond of posting a deluge of earnestly posed pictures of themselves on social media, with little thought of appearing vain or silly.

Romanians are a warm and tactile people. Their general friendliness and openness mean that they find some foreigners, particularly Northern Europeans, standoffish and cold by comparison. Do not be surprised if you consider yourself an affable person and a Romanian judges you as distant; they are merely applying the standards of their own society. People here are quick to extend the hand of friendship and cannot understand why some other nationalities don't do the same. Romanians are particularly friendly to foreigners (especially Westerners, who are appreciated for giving up the comforts of more developed societies in favor of Romania), and want these foreigners to form a good impression of their country. They are sometimes more reticent with compatriots, and foreign visitors occasionally find that people who have been enormously warm and welcoming to them can be slightly cooler if introduced to a Romanian partner or friend. (See below for a further exploration of this mistrust.)

Although many Romanians do settle in Germany and the UK, in general emigrants have a preference for Italy and Spain, countries where they feel more familiar with the language and behavior of the people. Some Romanian emigrants still target the US, particularly ambitious professionals in fields such as tech, medicine, and research. However, bureaucratic barriers to emigration, along with concerns about gun violence, healthcare costs, and, latterly, the Trump-era treatment of minorities—plus, of course, the issue of proximity, as Romanians—make visa-free and more culturally similar European countries a simpler and more appealing option. This is reflected in the numbers: both Spain and the UK are home to roughly three times as many Romanian-born residents as the US.

THE AFTERMATH OF COMMUNISM

Although it has been over thirty-five years since Communism officially ended in Romania, the country's near half century under the totalitarian regime has left an indelible impression on almost all aspects of life. Because the state was ubiquitous, influencing home as well as public life, traces of Communist thinking are evident in even the most personal issues, and are very difficult for some Romanians—particularly the older generation—to shake off. Many quirks regarding local beliefs and behavior can be traced back, at least in part, to the Soviet period.

No dissent or questioning of the system was permitted under Communism, and this instilled a conformity of thought and acceptance of authority that made Romania fertile ground for religious leaders and ad agencies after Communism. Because Romanians had not learned how to scrutinize, long-held beliefs and prejudices became difficult to shift. The education system emphasized—and still does, to an extent—rote learning over creativity and independent thought. Many people can fire off the names of capital cities with ease, but if asked to back up their opinions with reasoned arguments, they may flounder. Conformity is still prized to some extent, and individuality and diversity are viewed by many with suspicion, at least outside the metropolitan centers. Even something as innocuous as wearing slightly unusual clothes can attract strange looks, though this is changing as subgroups become established.

Another legacy is the poor standard of living conditions, services, and products. Interruptions to the hot water—or entire water supply—are not uncommon in residential blocks; neither are gas or power outages. While in the past many were resigned to this, growing civic consciousness and means of expression, combined with rising awareness of how utilities perform abroad, are encouraging Romanians to file complaints or at least vent about it on social media.

CUTTING CORNERS

Most Romanians grew up under a corrupt system, and trying to outsmart it in little ways became a way of life. Some people are quite ambivalent about dishonesty. There is even a word to describe unscrupulous behavior that earns a degree of admiration because of the élan with which it is executed: *şmecherie*. Cheating, cutting corners, and petty pilfering are not always met with the same disapproval as in Western society.

One cause is corruption in the education system, both under and since Communism, where struggling or lazy students could buy good grades through gifts to the (very underpaid) teacher, while able students who were unable or unwilling to do so were given poorer marks. This practice had the effect of severing the link between merit and actual grades, to the extent that for many, education was about doing what had to be done to attain the grades rather than learning and improving as a person. Many people have carried this mentality into their adult lives and even try to cheat on tests that go toward serious qualifications. Following greater oversight in the education system, this is now less prevalent, but rumors of teacher bribery persist, and parents often hire their child's teacher for extra lessons out of school hours both to help the child improve and to incur the teacher's favor.

This tolerance of cheating is evident in other aspects of life as well, such as the practice of fare evasion. It often appears incongruous that a moral, decent, sometimes religious Romanian will be quite blasé about such matters. It is important to remember that for decades, Romanians saw the *şmecheri* rise in power and wealth in their society, while honest folk remained mired in poverty. However, the jailing of some of the country's most seemingly untouchable politicians, media moguls, and businessmen, combined with the public indignation that followed a fatal nightclub fire in Bucharest in 2015 (blamed on corrupt safety officials who permitted the club to host an indoor pyrotechnic display), marked a change in the standard shoulder-shrugging response to corner cutting and cheating, boding well for the future.

CONSPICUOUS CONSUMPTION

In the 1990s, Romanians began celebrating their release from Communism by rebelling against its values. One of the most visible signs of this was the embrace of conspicuous consumption. This was quite understandable: for many years the country suffered great deprivation, denied the technological and aesthetic luxuries enjoyed by the West. In the years after the revolution, anything perceived as Western—symbolizing the opposite of everything the Romanian people had endured for so long—was pounced on, as Romanians enjoyed their first taste of capitalism and freedom (which became closely linked). Salaries were still not high, but with many young Romanians still living at home and therefore having few expenses, people were happy to splurge large portions of their salaries on securing the latest "must-have" (a term so popular, it has been co-opted into the Romanian language). Owning an $800 cell phone does not imply that someone has a $2,000 monthly salary; it's quite possible they make only $800 a month, and spent the entire paycheck on their phone.

Seeing the love of labels and tech, one could have reached the conclusion in those years that Romanian society was shallow and materialistic. This is overly harsh, however; the country was still in transition, and after years of poverty and restriction, most Romanians simply wanted to enjoy the pleasures—dressing up and owning nice things—that Westerners took for granted. Unencumbered by Western notions that showing off material possessions is vulgar, Romanians were relieved no longer to be so poor—and they weren't embarrassed about showing it.

In any case, conspicuous consumption is much less

noticeable now in the wake of the 2008 economic crisis, which gave the populace a sobering dose of realism about capitalism, and a drive to economize. At the same time, greater adoption of international mores mean many younger, more educated Romanians are becoming more understated in their style.

ATTITUDES TOWARD ETHNIC MINORITIES

Romania is not woke. Hearing amiable, educated Romanians airing their views on the local Roma population is likely to be one of the first-time foreign visitor's biggest culture shocks. A plainspoken people with little concept of political correctness, some Romanians may casually drop into the conversation such comments as, "I hate gypsies." Before denouncing them as irredeemable racists, however, it's important to try and understand the background of the tensions involved.

The Roma are a distinct racial group within the country, and while there is some integration, it remains limited. To some ethnic Romanian (who still often refers to the Roma by the term "gypsies"), much of the crime in the country is committed by these people. They are thought to control illegal activities such as drug trafficking, burglary, and prostitution; have a stranglehold on other, legal businesses such as flower selling; and indulge in price fixing and other unethical business practices. Many Romanians believe that the police allow Romani people to get away with things for which the authorities would come down hard on an ethnic Romanian. They also attribute much of the crime committed in the rest of Europe by Romanians to the Romani, and believe that foreigners see no difference between the two (owing in part to the similarity of the words), which leads them to the conclusion that the Roma are responsible for their country's bad reputation abroad, and the stigmatization that honest, hardworking Romanians face when they try to build a life elsewhere.

Of course, many people realize that part of what might drive a Romani to crime is lack of opportunities in the legitimate labor market—a result of the widespread discrimination they suffer—and that a vicious circle is in place. An aggravating factor is that most Romanians in the major towns are forced by the substandard Communist-era housing complexes to live in close proximity to each other. The typically communal Roma lifestyle does not go down well with neighbors living on the other side of a thin wall, and this ratchets up the enmity.

Romanians may speak disparagingly about immigrants from Southeast Asia, then complain in the same breath about xenophobic treatment of their own diaspora, unaware of the irony. Although it is increasingly rare, you may even hear people use the n-word with little idea of how offensive it is ("*negru*" is Romanian for black). Until quite recently, black and Asian visitors to Bucharest may have attracted stares. All of this came not from malice, but from the scarcity of people of a different ethnicity in the country, and lack of education about them. But in recent years, high numbers of immigrants have come, predominantly from Asia, to take up the type of jobs that Romanians moved westwards to do in their turn. Some universities also attract foreign students, particularly for medical degrees, which are much cheaper to complete in Romania than in Western Europe. Because of all this, members of ethnic minorities are becoming a more common sight, but in the smaller towns and villages the appearance of such a foreigner can still be something of an event.

That said, the Romanians' overriding impulse is often to welcome strangers to their country and home, and being of a different color is no barrier to making friends and being accepted into local groups. Indeed, the perceived glamor of "the exotic" can even help.

ATTITUDES TOWARD WESTERNERS

Although this phenomenon is easing as more Romanians get to travel abroad, Westerners—particularly white ones—still enjoy privilege. Whatever their view of the world outside Romania, most people love to make friends with visitors from the West. This seems to stem both from a desire to practice their language skills and to "access" the West by asking you about your home country and comparing your values and opinions to their own. As a foreigner, you'll get special dispensation in many different areas. Locals will refrain from much of the stronger criticism and bluntness they dish out to each other. Your opinion will be listened to and taken seriously. People will go all out to make a good impression. Some Romanians are still slightly in awe of foreigners, whom they believe to be rich, sophisticated, and influential. However, the much-mocked spectacle of young, attractive local women forming relationships with male expatriates of advancing years (and often waistlines) is less and less common. Rising salaries and falling borders mean more young Romanian women can head abroad under their own steam, making a foreign beau less of a necessity.

Ultimately, whether as a partner, a friend, a business colleague, or a stranger in the street, Romanians almost always go out of their way to make you feel welcome, valued, and at home.

ATTITUDES TOWARD AUTHORITY

Under Communism, any Romanian rebellion was brutally clamped down on, and people got used to doing what they were told, an attitude still seen to this day. Even figures with a very small amount of power—such as the administrators of old apartment complexes—could run a regime of fear, and would be very surprised if you did not comply with their every demand. At the same time, the malignant authoritarianism prompted people to find ways to circumvent the rules, which is also still in evidence.

Latter-day examples of blindly following authority include multinational corporations. Having had no exposure to modern advertising under Communism, Romanians had not developed the media literacy skills required to question the impressive-sounding claims of marketers. If it was on TV, some seemed to think, it must be true, though this attitude is changing with time and greater experience. Other modern authority figures include foreigners, who are often assumed to have superior knowledge and status, regardless of whether this is borne out in reality.

THE STATE VERSUS THE INDIVIDUAL

Perhaps the best example of the past attitude of the *nomenclatura* of the Romanian state is the People's Palace, the huge monstrosity built by Ceaușescu, second in size only to the Pentagon (and the largest civilian building in the world). Visible from almost all over the city, it looks down imposingly, dwarfing the individual as if to say, "We are the state." In the post-Communist period the state has become far more benign, but certain aspects of official behavior suggest some of its representatives still see themselves as authority figures first and public servants second. Examples of this attitude include the surly and

The Palace of the Parliament, Bucharest.

self-important demeanor of some civil servants and public officials, as well as the heavy-handed response to Covid-19, which saw even public parks shut and citizens obliged to bring a written declaration stating their business whenever they left home, under pain of a hefty fine.

PRIVACY AND PERSONAL SPACE

The hugely intrusive Communist state that controlled almost every facet of people's personal lives largely eroded the concept of privacy. Neighbors—particularly older ones—may take a prurient interest in each other's business. Don't be surprised if new acquaintances ask you some very direct questions about your salary, belief in God, marital status or intentions in this respect, or opinions on the Roma, gay rights, and other issues that might be conversational no-go areas in your home country. Again, this is not seen as prying or intended to make you feel uncomfortable—people just consider these legitimate discussion topics, and if they are curious about something, they will ask.

Personal space in Romania is also much less valued than you may be used to. Waiting in line was a big part of Communist life here, and unless one guarded one's position, someone else was liable to cut in; so older people have a tendency to stand very close to the person in front of them when waiting in line. The Latin ease of physical contact and closeness means that in cinemas, restaurants, and all forms of public transportation, other people are likely to sit much closer to you than you are used to, regardless of how many other free tables or seats there are. This is not necessarily an attempt to be rude or intimidating; many Romanians simply do not recognize the importance of personal space to others. After all, if the seat is free, why shouldn't they sit there? It is important to be aware of this, particularly if you are a woman; if you're sitting alone in an empty metro car and a man sits directly opposite you, this is not necessarily the potentially threatening situation it could be at home.

Perhaps the most obvious manifestation of the lack of regard for privacy is the staring you might experience. Many Romanians are in the habit of staring at anything or anyone they perceive as slightly different or interesting.

Because this is the norm, there is no taboo about looking intensely at someone, and if you eventually catch the person's eye they will feel no obligation to then avert their gaze, as would probably happen elsewhere. Nor are Romanians in the habit of breaking into a smile if there is prolonged eye contact. This can seem, to someone unused to it, to be an act of intimidation or hostility. It is seldom meant as such, but is merely curiosity. As a foreigner, your dress and demeanor can mark you out as unusual and you are likely to attract a few stares, but this is something visitors get used to if they stay for any length of time.

KEEPING A LOW PROFILE

Although its values are shifting irreversibly westward, Romania still has a collectivist culture more reminiscent of the East than of Western individualism. Membership in a group—be it family, friends, or workmates—is often expected to take priority over one's individual wants and needs. On top of that, the predominantly working-class culture of the cities brought by the rural dwellers moved en masse by Ceaușescu emphasizes community solidarity over self-betterment. The result is that those who seek to improve themselves can sometimes meet resistance (aside from by getting richer, which everyone understands). Away from the cosmopolitan young urbanites who have embraced the wellness messages emanating from the West, lifestyle improvements such as jogging, quitting smoking, or cutting down on red meat can baffle some people, who perhaps construe such desires in others as a rejection of their values.

Romanian society also has an element of *schadenfreude*, summed up by a joke in which a Romanian is granted any wish imaginable by a genie and replies, "I wish my neighbor's goat would die." Some people may cagily refuse to cede any advantage, such as not slowing down to allow a pedestrian to nip across the street, even if they have a red light ahead anyway and it would cost them nothing. The flip side of all of this is the strong solidarity of local communities.

MEN AND WOMEN

Gender roles in Romania are more rigid than the Western visitor might be used to: in 2024, the country ranked last in the EU's Gender Equality Index. Very few women are solely homemakers—hardly any families could afford this—but apart from the most modern couples, the majority of domestic and child-rearing duties are still performed by the woman. There are strict ideas about ideal masculine traits—strength, dominance, being a good provider—and feminine traits—being submissive, gentle, and sexually attractive—and people who contravene the norm may meet resistance and disapproval. In more traditional, working-class Romanian families, it is accepted that the husband is the boss, and some men may address their wives in abrupt tones that might surprise a foreigner. Women, particularly older ones, may be quite submissive to their husbands.

Domestic violence remains a serious problem in Romania. Forty-two percent of women have experienced physical and/or sexual violence since the age of 15, 11 percentage points higher than the EU average, according to statistics from 2024. Legislative efforts to change mentalities have been patchy. Echoes of the #MeToo movement were seen in 2024, when several high-profile academics were accused of abusing female students. During his campaign, 2025 presidential candidate George Simion told a female senator, "*Te agresez sexual, scroafo!*"—which roughly translates to "I'll sexually assault you, you cow!"—during a filmed scuffle. (He lost the election, but only by a small margin.) Outside the home, some men (both urbane and traditional) insist that doors should be held open for women. Restaurant bills are often automatically presented to the man, and in some more formal establishments male waiters may still help a woman on with her coat.

While women make up much of the workforce, they are more poorly paid for the low-skilled jobs they traditionally hold compared to equivalent jobs held by men. A few high-profile exceptions notwithstanding—then USR president Elena Lasconi made the second round of the subsequently annulled presidential election in 2024—women are still underrepresented in the higher echelons of Romanian business and politics. Part of this is due to the lingering view that a woman's chief value is her physical appearance. The EU has criticized the sexist presentation of women in the media in the past—and while things have improved significantly, skimpily attired women appear on everything from casino adverts to bottles of antiseptic. This has seeped into the general Romanian mentality, and many men cannot understand why a woman would not be flattered to be stared at and commented on as she passes on the street. Indeed, a minority of local woman do seem to welcome and encourage this kind of attention, although the stereotype of the *pițipoancă* (the word translates approximately to bimbo) is becoming a rarer sight as fashion styles move closer to Western norms.

Many Romanians, particularly the better educated ones, find the feminine ideal held up in their country extremely frustrating. While feminism was originally largely discredited by its association with Communism, the voices arguing for women's rights in Romania today are becoming more audible, and some NGOs dedicated to the issue have sprung up in the past decade or so. As a foreigner, you are likely to be spared much of the worst discrimination; nationality seems to trump gender in Romanian perceptions.

Attitudes to sexual activity before marriage have changed in line with the rest of Europe. While the ideal among the older generation was to wait until one was married before having sex, the majority of younger people are far more in tune with modern liberal values. Few but the most devout or naive parents would expect their children to be virgins on their wedding night.

Most Romanians still take a traditional binary view of gender, often scoffing at the international discourse around trans rights and pronouns, which remains extremely niche outside the most progressive urban circles.

SUSPICION

It is estimated that the Communists had a network of 400,000 to 700,000 informers, equating to between 2 and 4 percent of the population, including several in every single apartment block in the country. This frightening statistic made suspicion a necessary self-defense mechanism for the average Romanian. This is perhaps one reason why many Romanians do not extend the same warm and open welcome to their compatriots that they do to foreigners, and people are liable to assume the worst of others. Unlike most foreigners, Romanians still sometimes fear that a compatriot might have a cousin or neighbor working in a governmental department that could make life difficult for them if they fell out of favor.

Suspicion has also contributed to the country's nepotism: people are often more willing to enter into a relationship, either business or personal, with someone to whom they are connected in some way (a relative or a friend of a friend) than a complete stranger. Expatriates and visitors often notice that local people who have been enormously helpful and friendly to them may clam up when a fellow Romanian is involved.

PASSIVITY AND FATALISM

Romanians were pretty much powerless during their four decades of Communist rule. The regime crushed civic spirit, and even after freedom of speech was theoretically restored, people were used to bearing their misfortunes and deprivations stoically and not protesting or complaining via the channels provided. The phrase "*Asta e*," meaning "That's the way it is," summed up this feeling of impotence and resignation. However, this is changing as civil society finally burgeons. Younger generations are more likely to make their voices heard, be it complaining about poor services or at political demonstrations. The larger cities see well-attended protests and marches, whether against corruption scandals, for minority rights, or for or against a particular candidate.

HOSPITALITY

It is hard to think of more generous hosts than Romanians. No matter how poor the people welcoming you into their home are, they will give you the very best of what they have. Out will come the best meat, and more food and drink than you could ever manage to consume. Neither your plate nor your glass will remain empty for long, as seconds and thirds are proffered regardless of whether you're still hungry or thirsty. It is best to accept graciously if possible.

The Little Ewe

Romanians' tendency toward fatalism is neatly summed up in "The Little Ewe," one of the country's most enduring pastoral tales. The ewe in question, named Miorița, tells her young master that two of his fellow shepherds are planning to murder him and split his assets. Instead of escaping or outwitting his would-be assailants, as a Western story would surely demand, the shepherd accepts his fate and instead sets about planning his funeral. Romanian writers and thinkers have presented various positive interpretations of the story, but few foreigners can view the shepherd's attitude as anything other than unfathomably pessimistic.

If you're eating out, the host—usually the most senior male of the party—will traditionally foot the bill, regardless of protestations. This can be awkward, as the oldest man is not always the highest earner, and the foreign visitor may feel it unfair for him to cover the expenses of a group night out. A foreigner is unlikely to be allowed to play host, however—the locals will consider it their duty to treat you—so there's little that can be done about it without offending someone's pride. Among younger groups, however, dividing the bill based on consumption is more common.

MONEY

Unlike some parts of the Western world, there is nothing embarrassing or vulgar about money in Romania. It is not considered crass or intrusive to ask someone's salary or reveal one's own. In a restaurant, locals may debate how much to tip directly in front of the staff—which can be mortifying for any foreigners present—and then directly give the staff the money while paying the bill, rather than the Western tradition of discreetly leaving it on the table before exiting.

Many Romanians take pride in owning and showing off expensive things, and people are far more likely to spend their money on items that others will see, such as clothes, cars, and gadgets. A Romanian in a top-of-the-line foreign car often drives home to a relatively modest apartment, while someone who drinks an expensive imported beer in a club will go home and drink the cheapest local brand.

Social class and money are tightly correlated. When local people speak of the "middle class," they are not referring to someone who is well educated, lives in a suburb, or has certain refined tastes and values—they mean it strictly from a monetary sense. A millionaire will be considered to be of a high social class no matter how boorish their tastes and behavior. Romanian reverence for money may seem crass, but having been deprived of it for so long, people enjoy what money they have without shame.

RELIGION

Although Romania is officially a secular state, the vast majority of people—73.6 percent in the 2021 Census—consider themselves members of the Romanian Orthodox Church (a significant drop from the 86.5 percent of ten years earlier, which is partly attributable to immigration). The remainder is made up of Protestants (6.3%), Roman Catholics (3.9%), those citing secular beliefs or no religion (0.8%), and the Romanian-Greek Catholic Church (0.6%). There are also small Muslim and Jewish communities. Many Romanians simultaneously interpret the Bible literally and accept the theory of evolution without seeing any inconsistency.

Religious symbols are common: families often have icons in their homes, and many taxi drivers hang crosses over their rearview mirrors. Whether this denotes great piety is another matter. Although a high proportion of Romanians will cross themselves when they pass a church, actual church attendance is far lower, with various surveys suggesting that only between 15 and 30 percent of Romanians go at least once a week. Celebrations such as Easter and Christmas do draw bigger congregations. Religion is not considered a taboo subject, and you may be questioned about your position.

The Communist regime did its best to marginalize religion, bulldozing churches and synagogues. Today religion is not under threat from the state but from the larger European trend toward secularism. For example, state funding for new churches has been met with public outrage, with a notable example being the grandiose People's Salvation Cathedral begun in 2010 near the People's Palace in Bucharest and consecrated in 2018. As in other countries, younger Romanians are less devout than their parents, and urban dwellers less so than rural communities. Some older people still avoid labor on Sundays, such as doing the laundry.

SUPERSTITION

Alongside religion, strong beliefs also have a hold on Romanian life in the form of superstition. This is much stronger in the countryside, where people are less educated and their lives more dependent on the whims of nature, so anything they can do to encourage good luck, they will. Spilling salt on the table is considered unlucky, but this can be offset if the spiller puts some of it on their forehead. Salt is sometimes thrown in the middle of a storm to try to end it. Dropping certain things (cutlery, matches) heralds an auspicious visit or good luck. Brides should not see each other in church—because weddings are concentrated around certain times of the year for religious reasons, there may be many ceremonies on the same day—and siblings should not marry in the same year. A bouquet of flowers given as a present should consist of an odd number; an even number is the norm for funerals. Belief in horoscopes is widespread, even among educated and professional Romanians.

One of the superstitions (though it is considered medical fact by many) most likely to impact on you is the phobia of moving air, known as *curent*. Many Romanians believe that fans, air-conditioning, and drafts are harmful, responsible for every ailment from a cold to a toothache to meningitis. They cannot bear to sit in a room with both the window and the door open, and would rather endure sweltering heat. This can be immensely frustrating if you share a hot office with local colleagues. Unfortunately, logic-based attempts to convince anyone that moving air is safe and pleasant seldom work, and other explanations for conditions (such as attributing toothaches to poor dental hygiene) are usually dismissed. Even occasional articles in the press by doctors, assuring readers that moving air is not the cause of hordes of maladies, fail to dent the belief. The standard hospitable deference to a foreigner's wishes may persuade your host to leave the window open and allow you a bit of a breeze on a hot day, but the fear is so entrenched that it is usually not long until someone rushes over in a panic to close it to stop the draft. While, prior to the advent of the coronavirus, this was a bizarre quirk of local lore at which foreigners generally chuckled, it became a serious issue during the pandemic, when many Romanians' fears of the mythical harms of moving air exposed them and others to the real ills of the virus, even as they still insisted on keeping office, train, and bus windows firmly shut.

CHAPTER THREE

CUSTOMS & TRADITIONS

Owing to their propensity for collective behavior, customs and traditions are important to Romanians. During the bleak years of Communism, public holidays, birthdays, and weddings were among the rare occasions when people could relax and enjoy themselves, and they are celebrated with much revelry and fanfare. People typically keep to tried and trusted ways of passing holidays and celebrating events. Alcohol often features significantly.

PUBLIC HOLIDAYS

Public holidays are much looked forward to in Romania, with discussions and plans about what to do starting several weeks in advance. Because people tend to stick to traditional activities and timeworn customs, you can expect certain places to be very busy on public holidays, namely parks (providing the weather is good) and resorts (coastal in warm weather, mountains throughout the year). Various forms of civic entertainment, such as free concerts or family events in parks, are frequently organized around these days.

If public holidays fall midweek, the day off is often shifted to make a long weekend. This is done to avoid disrupting the workweek, either by the state or by companies themselves.

PUBLIC HOLIDAYS

New Year (*Anul nou*): January 1 and 2

Orthodox Easter Sunday and Monday (*Paștele*): Various

Labor Day (*Ziua muncii*): May 1

National or Union Day (*Ziua națională* or *Ziua Unirii*): December 1 (celebrating the union of Transylvania with the Kingdom of Romania in 1918, the foundation of the modern state. It is commemorated with a large military parade attended by political leaders, speeches, and the switching on of the Christmas lights).

Christmas Eve (*Ajunul Crăciunului*): December 24

Christmas (*Craciun*): December 25 and 26

OTHER OFFICIAL HOLIDAYS AND OBSERVANCES

First day of spring (*Mărțișorul*): March 1

International Women's Day (*Ziua Internațională a femeii*): March 8

Heroes' Day or Ascension Day (*Ziua Eroilor* or *Înălțarea*): The 40th day after Easter

Flag Day (*Ziua Tricolorului*): June 26

Constitution Day (*Ziua Constituției*): December 6

FAMILY OCCASIONS

Christmas

Romanian Christmas celebrations are not dissimilar to festivities in Western countries. Things do get started a little earlier, on St. Nicholas's Day on December 6; on this day, children's boots, which have been polished and left out the night before, are traditionally filled with small presents from *Moş Nicolae* (Old Man Nicholas, not to be confused with the Western "Saint Nick" as an alternative name for Santa). The addition of a stick to warn the little ones to behave well for the year ahead has become less common. In the run-up to the day itself, carols (*colinde*) are sung at schools and at neighbors' doorways, and many places celebrate with a party. Santa Claus, known

Christmas decorations in a snow-covered Brasov.

Dancers and musicians take part in a traditional Christmas parade in the city of Bacău.

as *Moş Crăciun* (Old Man Christmas, a different person than Old Man Nicholas) comes on Christmas Eve, with another round of presents.

The more elaborate traditions are observed in the villages, however. Pork is the customary Christmas meat. Villagers normally buy a pig, if they don't already have one, and slit its throat in their backyard before dismembering it for meat. (The EU granted Romania's festive porcine dispatching a dispensation from bloc rules on animal slaughter.) Whatever is edible is eaten over the Christmas period, including the skin (*şorici*), which is lightly toasted and eaten then and there. The pork meat lasts throughout the holiday and is served up in different forms, including *sarmale* (cabbage leaves stuffed with rice, pork, and vegetables), with city dwellers often getting their share from relatives in the country.

Many people attend church on Christmas Eve, which is also the time when some put up and decorate the tree—although as elsewhere, some people choose to do this earlier, as well as shops, bars, and restaurants. As in many countries, the next day is a family affair, consisting of the main opening of presents (which usually takes a fair amount of time, owing to the quantity of gifts) and a huge meal. The next few days are spent eating and relaxing. While some companies do not require their staff to return until the new year, others are open for the last few days of December. Some festive lights and decorations can be seen brightening the winter mood well into January or even beyond.

New Year's Eve

While Christmas is a time for family, seeing the new year in is more about friends. Romanians will have parties or go drinking in bars, restaurants, and nightclubs, with festivities continuing until 5:00 or 6:00 a.m. Midnight

The traditional bear dance at the end of the year, here seen in Botosani.

firework displays are popular in the towns. Previously, these often focused on the aesthetic element to the detriment of health and safety concerns, and could be quite terrifying; however, following greater regulation, revelers can now walk the streets more at ease, although should still beware of the odd stray firework.

Easter

Easter is the most important festival in the Orthodox Christian year, and many émigrés will head home to celebrate it with relatives. Chief among its traditions is the painting, breaking, and eating of eggs. Boiled eggs are colored, and then smashed against each other, as the smashers say "Christ is risen" (*Hristos a înviat*) and "He is risen indeed" (*Adevărat a înviat*) in a traditional game. Other festive food includes lamb and a sweetbread called *cozonac*. Christians attend church on Easter Saturday evening for the Night of Resurrection (*Noapte de Înviere*) service, with many staying there all night. Part of the ceremony sees the priest light candles held by members of the congregation, who then do the same until everybody's candles are lit. Known as "taking the light," this is a pleasant and pretty tradition to take part in and witness.

Name Days

Many Romanians name their children after saints. On the particular day associated with a given saint, people who share the name will celebrate in much the same manner as they would their birthday. Children will bring sweets into school for their classmates, and if a few adults are celebrating together—some name days coincide—there may be a small work party. People also celebrate on the saint's day of their middle name.

Other Special Days

Early March is a good time to be a Romanian flower seller. March 1, officially the first day of spring, is known as *Mărțișorul*. Men traditionally give flowers or small gifts to all the women with whom they will have dealings that day; boys distribute them to female teachers and classmates. A small red and white lanyard is attached to the bunch, which the woman then pins on her clothing for luck. One week later the florists are busy again, for International Women's Day.

FROM BIRTH TO DEATH

Babies are often named after a close relative, or given the name of the saint whose day is closest to their birthday. Most are given two first names. A typical name would be Andreea Maria Ionescu, or Ion (John) Andrei (Andrew) Popescu. The core list of Romanian names is fairly limited and well used, and traditionally there were very few cases (outside the Roma community) of parents departing from the norm and imaginatively giving their offspring an unusual, foreign, or invented name, although that is

A priest preparing for a baptism in Timișoara.

changing as young and educated Romanians become more international in outlook. A newborn baby will usually be baptized within its first few months of life. The event will often be a big one, attended by the parents' family and friends and followed by a party. A couple is usually chosen to be the child's godparents. In an odd quirk, parents will often address their offspring by their own title—a mother will call her child *mama/mami* (mom/mommy) and a father *tata/tati* (dad/daddy).

Birthdays are big events for Romanians, even sometimes for adults, offering a chance to forget the travails of daily life and celebrate among friends. If the party is held in a restaurant or bar, the custom is for the person whose birthday it is to pay for all the food and drink consumed. This might explain why not everyone chooses to celebrate their birthday! Guests are expected to bring presents, and flowers if the person celebrating is a woman.

A wedding is a huge deal in the life of most Romanians, who will probably have been encouraged to take this step by their parents for most of their lives. A civil ceremony, attended by close friends and family only, is followed later that day, or soon after, by a church service, after which a restaurant is booked for a big party. Instead of bringing presents, guests are expected to give cash (envelopes are often provided)—enough to cover their share of the cost (*tacâm*) plus some extra. Some foreigners—and even some Romanians themselves—find this practice somewhat mercenary, and think it distorts the happy spirit of the occasion. For example, some couples invite rich acquaintances to the exclusion of closer but less wealthy friends. Indeed, while theoretically the couple should

A wedding party in traditional costumes, Vama.

be happy for a poor friend to attend, even if he or she is unable to donate any money, in practice this is not always the case, and sometimes people will skip a wedding for financial reasons. Not every couple can afford to pay for elaborate wedding costs, though, so the system does allow less affluent couples to marry without shouldering a large debt. These days, as newlyweds get older and more solvent, some modern couples are willing and able to finance their nuptials themselves, and are therefore more relaxed if guests give a gift in lieu of cash.

The Romanian version of a wedding reception involves traditions such as the kidnapping of the bride, where male guests take the bride a short distance away and return her in exchange for a "ransom," usually alcohol. Newlyweds also choose godparents—an older married couple who can give them advice—when they get married. Unlike in countries like the US or UK, the role of godparents in Romania is symbolic and spiritual rather than legal. Godparents don't adjust their wills to reflect their role, nor would they be expected to assume guardianship of a child if something happened to the parents. (This duty would typically default to the grandparents, who have traditionally played a central role in raising grandchildren.) Dowries have effectively disappeared outside some rural and Roma communities.

As elsewhere, declining religiosity, women's greater earning power, and more modern mentalities are seeing more couples eschew matrimony, but marriage rates are still among the highest in the EU. Civil partnerships—

whether for same-sex or different-sex couples—are not recognized.

Funeral customs are another area of traditional Romanian life altered by EU membership. While in the past it was traditional for the body to lie in an open casket in the home for three days after death, EU regulations mean that this now mostly happens in a chapel, although the practice persists in rural areas. After the church service, at which mourners approach the casket and say good-bye to the deceased—often rather emotionally—the body is buried. This is followed by some food, either at the cemetery or later at the house of the bereaved family, or a nearby restaurant. The family often give alms (*pomană*), consisting of parcels of food and sometimes crockery, to mourners and neighbors.

Coliva, a boiled wheat dish associated with funerals.

CHAPTER **FOUR**

MAKING FRIENDS

To a Romanian, a true friend is an extension of the family, a person to welcome into your home and with whom to share confidences, possessions, and even money, when necessary. Returning expatriates often complain that friendship outside Romania is colder and more distant—for example, that non-Romanians prefer you to call ahead or schedule gatherings in advance rather than just drop by. In practice, though, many Romanians prefer their friends to phone ahead as well.

Because Romanian society is so couple-centric, as we will see further on, friendship can take a backseat for some once they find a partner. While middle-aged socializing tends to occur often in sets of couples, single-sex or mixed groups of friends do spend evenings together, especially in the larger cities. The "boys' night out," however, is still more common than the "girls' night out." In times of need, people are more likely to turn first to their immediate family or their partner.

As well as school, college, and work, the local area also provides a significant source of acquaintances, and many friendship groups are composed largely of neighbors. (As elsewhere, rural or working-class Romanians often socialize with relatives and neighbors, while middle-class or urban ones tend to do so more with friends.) Owing in large part to the suspicion fostered by the Communist system, adult Romanians have traditionally tended not to make new friends that easily, and their social circles are made up of just a few people whom they have known a long time. This is changing, however, and this wariness does not extend to foreigners, who are pretty much guaranteed a warm welcome.

While making friends usually happens fairly quickly, it can take longer to adjust to Romanian manners, which can seem absent on occasions. People can be disarmingly direct, talk in loud, aggressive-sounding tones, interrupt, and seldom bother with a "please" or "thank you." It is better to get used to things before passing judgment: what initially seems like rudeness or boorishness often has an explanation, or is simply not considered bad manners in Romania. Once you have adjusted to this, your dealings with people will become much more pleasant.

HOW TO MEET PEOPLE

Romanians are friendly and open, particularly to foreigners, and you should have no trouble meeting people. Bars and nightclubs are standard places to meet others. Coworkers

Friends at a street food stall, Cluj-Napoca.

often do some socializing together, so you are likely to get to know any colleagues reasonably well. Conversations can even spring up on public transportation, especially long train journeys, in shops, in parks, in playgrounds, and on the street; in short, in many places a foreign accent will be enough to get you noticed and engaged in conversation. The internet and social media are the new vanguard of socializing, in the big cities at least, and there are various expatriate groups and meet-ups that publicize themselves and their activities on Facebook, InterNations being one such. Embassies' events are also hubs for their own nationals and often the wider international community too. Certain activities open to all—such as pub quizzes and darts leagues—are also very social, and tend to have a strong expatriate component. Romanian society is network-based, with introductions and friends of friends facilitating a lot of business and personal connections. Once you make one friend, it is a small step to integrating into a whole bunch. The still limited extent of the expatriate community means that you will quickly get to know fellow foreigners, and everybody seems to know everybody else in one way or another. In rural communities, integration may be more challenging, but people are still often friendly if you persist.

FORMS OF ADDRESS

Traditional etiquette required that a younger person greet an older person first, although few people still have this expectation. The convention is that a child should greet an adult, and a man a woman, by saying "*Sãrut-mâna*," which translates as "I kiss your hand." The old-school gents who would accompany this with the described action and actually kiss the woman's hand are now a rarity.

Time was when men would shake hands with other men present, and theoretically acknowledge the women with a nod and a "hello" of some form (but in practice totally ignore them, a snub with which many Romanian women, used to their lower standing in society, seemed to find nothing amiss). This is less common now, although some more traditional men may still feel uncomfortable shaking hands with a woman. The double kiss on the cheek (with no gender restriction) on arrival and departure is typical among closer friends and family, or people meeting again after a long time. Young female friends sometimes hold hands in the street, which young men would never be seen doing.

Interestingly, given that Romania is generally a tactile country, hugging isn't always the default gesture of affection, and even an emotionally wrought, tearful parent greeting a returning child may do so with a double cheek kiss rather than a warm embrace—though younger Romanians are often less standoffish in this respect.

Like greetings, terms of address vary. Friends and colleagues who know each other well generally use each other's first names, or sometimes surnames in an informal, jovial way. With people with whom they are less familiar, they might precede their first name with Mr. or Mrs. (*Domnul* or *Doamna*). These terms can also be used before someone's profession, as in *Domnul director* for "Mr. Director."

Like other Latin languages, Romanian has a formal and an informal way of addressing people, the former also being used in the plural. The single informal word for "you" is *tu*, the plural *voi*, and the formal *dumneavoastră*. These pronouns are seldom actually spoken, however; rather, the form of the verb used indicates which pronoun is implied. For example, "you are" (informal, singular) is *tu ești,* but it is normally expressed simply as *ești,* and *voi* or *dumneavoastră sunteți* expressed just as *sunteți.* This can be awkward for foreigners unfamiliar with the system, faced with the dilemma of risking impertinence or implying an unfriendly distance. In general, the polite form *dumneavoastră* is used to someone of higher "status"—a category that includes older people and those in seniority at work or in a social situation—and the informal version *tu* for people of the same age or younger or in an inferior social position. This causes obvious incongruities. What if a shop assistant or waiter—a social "inferior"—is much older than you? On top of that, some people use the polite form when meeting any new person, except a child, for the first time, and expect the same in return. Serious arguments have been known to result from disputes over the wrong form of address, though the general discourse is becoming more casual over time.

Fortunately, foreigners have some leeway, and Romanians do not expect an outsider to be familiar with the convention. If in doubt, stick to the formal version—a Romanian who wants to deal with you on a friendlier and more relaxed basis will soon let you know.

TABLE MANNERS

The table manners of the average Romanian family may seem a little rough-hewn to an outsider. As we have seen, many urban Romanians have parents from the countryside, and often it is a case of rustic country ways looking a little uncouth in the city. Meals are often jovial, informal occasions, with few feeling the need to stand on ceremony. Family members rarely wait until the cook—in most cases the mother—is seated before they start eating, and will often dig in as soon as they receive their portion. People may eat quite noisily and deposit bones and the like on the table itself. The upside of this is that Romanians tend to be relaxed about manners and etiquette in others, and you're unlikely to offend by using the wrong knife.

Expect to be offered seconds and even thirds. Refusals are usually interpreted as politeness rather than honest expressions of preference, and your host is likely to persist until you yield. Do not expect that asking for a little will make any difference to the amount you are given. It's important to compliment the food; for extra brownie points you can compare it favorably with the same dish you've eaten elsewhere. Many Romanians fervently insist (and genuinely believe) that their own mother makes the best sarmale, cozonoc, etc., and to do anything but concur would be the gravest faux pas. Toasts are common, and there may be several throughout the course of the meal. When toasting, Romanians say "good luck" (*noroc*) or "to your health" (*sanatate)*. They also use the same words after somebody sneezes, which is why some Romanians might say "cheers" to an English-speaker who has sneezed!

SMOKING

Romania is a smoking country by tradition. A large proportion of people smoke here compared to the West—34 percent according to a recent survey—and attitudes toward the habit are very different. There has been little compunction about lighting up around non-smokers without asking permission (excepting in the home of a non-smoker). People would smoke while others were eating, in elevators, and—perhaps the most upsetting to witness—around children, regardless of the obvious discomfort of others. Until fairly recently, some offices still allowed smoking.

However, with greater assimilation with and travel to the West, and awareness of healthy lifestyles, the habit began to fall from favor among more educated young Romanians. Nonsmoking sections sprang up in the more upmarket hotels and restaurants, and a few pioneers—often trendy, Western-style cafés—took the commercially brave step of going totally smoke-free.

The fatal fire in Colectiv nightclub in October 2015, although not caused by a cigarette, focused public attention on health and safety issues. Against all odds—and opposition from big tobacco—lawmakers voted for a ban on smoking in public places, which came into force on March 16, 2016.

Don't expect to escape the fumes entirely, though: some restaurants and bars have found loopholes in the form of semi-covered terraces, while some Romanian apartment blocks are so poorly constructed and ventilated that smoke sometimes wafts from one dwelling to another via various pipes and gaps. In less formal workplaces, smokers may still sneak a crafty puff in the kitchen.

CONVERSATION

We have seen that if Romanians are interested in something, they will ask you about it. They also feel free to voice their own opinions, some of which may veer toward the politically incorrect. There is a saying that if you have three Romanians at a table, you will have four different opinions. Romanians enjoy a good argument, although they often argue with passion and received wisdom rather than facts and intellectual rigor. Feel free to voice your own views, but don't expect to convert anyone to your

Outdoor dinner among friends, Sibiu.

way of thinking, regardless of any watertight arguments you might produce. Despite the general lack of conversational taboos, Romanians may be quite shocked if you admit to drug taking or state openly that you are gay; their respect for foreigners will probably override that, however, and a lively debate should engender no bad feelings.

Other people are often a major topic of conversation. Whose son or daughter has gone to work abroad, who's in poor health, who's got a new job, house, or car, who's getting married, plus any anecdotes that illustrate the terrible state of society today, may all be shared. While better-educated and more well-traveled Romanians are likely to ply you with questions about your homeland, others will have very local horizons and may exhibit a very limited interest in the world outside their country, considering it of little relevance to their lives.

Romanians often love a full and frank political debate. The performance of football teams or other national sporting icons, celebrity and political scandals, and the (poor) state of the local services/infrastructure and who is to blame are often analyzed. The outrageous, spiraling prices are always a hot topic. You may be asked your zodiac sign and then told who, among your interlocutor's circle, shares it.

Conversations are often conducted in a loud, informal manner. It is quite common for people to interrupt regularly and speak over each other, and this is not considered rude. If someone feels contempt for what another person has said, they will feel no compunction in showing it, and many people use a wide array of interjections, facial expressions, and noises to convey their views. Opinions are stated directly and seldom cushioned with kind words, although, as usual, many Romanians are aware that outsiders may not be used to such bluntness and will soften their speech accordingly. Many people feel free to change the subject suddenly, rather than observe a few moments' silence to check that nobody has anything to add before doing so.

Joining in a conversation in the Romanian language can be tough, even if you have some knowledge of it. Because interaction with foreigners on Romanian soil is a relatively new phenomenon, people here—especially older or less-travelled ones—can find it difficult to remember to speak slowly and use simple words. This is especially true if you are talking to more than one Romanian speaker, as the pace of the conversation will immediately pick up. Even when the language used is your own, it can be hard to break in and make your voice heard. The best idea is to abandon much of what you were taught as a child and to feel at liberty to butt in, cut people off, and talk over them when they try to do the same to you. This can be a huge social challenge, but otherwise you are likely to spend group outings contributing relatively little to the conversation.

Street-based conversations are often concluded as the participants are separating, so good-byes may be exchanged by shouting over a distance of several meters.

EDUCATION AND OPINIONS

Are Romanians well educated? Yes and no. The Communist emphasis on education has worked its way into received wisdom, but in Romania it applied to a certain kind of education only. Because the Ceauşescu regime wanted prestigious engineering and infrastructure projects to prove to the world the greatness of Communism, it needed workers capable of constructing them—it did not want its citizens developing inquiring minds or too much independent thought. The education system, therefore, taught certain skills, problem-solving techniques, and behavior, without encouraging people to think very much for themselves. It could be argued that the regime wanted its people well trained rather than well educated.

The effects of this are evident today—indeed, something of it remains in classrooms. Reformers are still fighting an uphill battle to modernize the public education system: the rote learning and copying out of page after page of letters, which has echoes of 1950s education in Western schools, alongside the presence of Orthodox Christianity taught as fact, dismay many progressive parents. While Romania produces highly competent linguists and software programmers—disciplines that require one to learn rules and operate within them—the creative professions still lag behind (some impressive and internationally acclaimed filmmaking notwithstanding). Many young Romanians display excellent general knowledge—for example, plenty can recite famous poems by heart—but are on shakier ground if asked to justify their own opinions or think critically or creatively. Hearing foreigners assert and defend their views, particularly unorthodox ones, can unduly impress some Romanians.

On some everyday topics, however, Romanians will almost always express an opinion rather than admit ignorance on a subject. Do not assume that because advice is presented with confidence, the person offering it has any evidence or experience to back up their viewpoint. The mind control practiced by the Communist regime suppressed any inclination to challenge the received wisdom, and once people get an idea fixed in their minds, little can dislodge it and they will voice it repeatedly and with full certainty. If you get to know Romanians very well, you may also find that they have opinions on the most private and intimate minutiae of other people's lives—even regarding matters you would not consider possible for people to have opinions on, such as on which side a person should sleep in their bed.

As in other domains, things are changing with greater travel opportunities and exposure to international media: the above traits are less visible in younger, urban, and educated Romanians embracing the ongoing march of Western values.

It is worth noting that when Romanians use the term "well educated," they are typically not referring to someone's school and university attainments; rather, they're saying that the person is polite, civilized, and well brought up, a concept they also refer to as "*cei şapte ani de acasă*," literally the seven years at home.

LANGUAGE

Young Romanians—especially cosmopolitan ones—often have excellent foreign language skills. Immersed in American and Western culture through music, TV, film, and the internet, they have a constant supply of English to absorb and speak it instinctively and confidently. They are also extremely well motivated, keenly aware that to work or study abroad, rise up the ranks in a multinational company in Romania, or go into business, English skills are usually vital. Many people are very keen to practice English with a native speaker—but there's a caveat. While speaking English to nonnative English speakers, Romanians are relatively relaxed about making errors; aware that a native speaker will notice all their mistakes, however, some of them—especially older ones—feel embarrassed and are subsequently reluctant to talk. They seem unaware of the irony that their interlocutor's proficiency in Romanian is likely to be minimal, and that they will probably be impressed by the level of English they have achieved, regardless of any mistakes. Increasingly, many young Romanians speak English even when speaking Romanian! Hip Gen Zs like to pepper their Romanian conversations with English words and phrases, to the chagrin of (usually older) language purists. Examples include "*Ne-am dus la party și era super chill*" ("We went to the party and it was super chill") or "*E o întrebare așa random, dar whatever*" ("It's such a random question, but whatever").

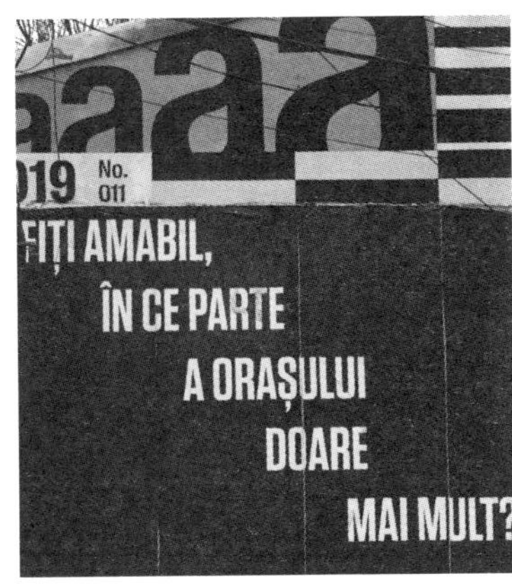

Billboard with spray-painted graffiti, Bucharest.

With older Romanians, usually from around fifty-five upward, the situation is different. People of this generation, schooled in the Communist era, were taught Russian and French, not English, and strict censorship laws denied them access to English-language radio, TV, and media. The upshot of this is that in this age group, English is spoken at a lower and less natural level. Many individuals and companies have tried to remedy this, with business English lessons proving very popular as multinational companies moved in; but above a certain age, few people (apart from those who have had the opportunity to travel or study abroad) will have any degree of fluency, and to converse with them you will have to make the effort to learn some Romanian, or use a translation app.

Learning Romanian

Although Romanian is a Latin language—so already knowing any French, Spanish, or Italian will help—and phonetic, with simple spelling, its grammar makes it difficult to master. Another obstacle is the response you will get to your efforts. Romanians are not at all disparaging of foreigners' attempts to learn the lingo—on the contrary, they are supportive and delighted to hear your mangled sentences—but because their country was closed off to outsiders under Communism, their experience of non-Romanians speaking the language was practically nonexistent, at least until the wave of immigration predominantly from Asia over the last decade or so. Whereas any English speaker is used to hearing English spoken in numerous accents and with varying degrees of accuracy, this is something novel to Romanians, and their first instinct is to laugh. This is from delight rather than derision, but it can be rather off-putting, as can the tendency of fluent English speakers to reply to your efforts in English. Their lack of exposure to hearing their language spoken in different accents can also mean that Romanians are prevented from understanding you by the slightest discrepancy in pronunciation—though, again, this is changing as the country is exposed to a fledgling multiculturalism.

Despite this, the average Romanian will greatly appreciate your labors, and learning the language is usually a rewarding endeavor, giving you access to people and culture that you would otherwise be denied.

HELPFUL PHRASES

Hello: *Salut, bunâ*

Goodbye: *La revedere*

How are you?: *Ce (mai) faci?*

Fine, thank you: *Mulţumesc, bine*

Pleased to meet you: *Incântat / Îmi pare bine*

Good morning: *Bună dimineaţa*

Good day: *Bună ziua*

Good evening: *Bună seara*

Good night: *Noapte bună*

Yes: *Da*

No: *Nu*

Please: *Vă rog*

Thank you: *Mulţumesc*

I'm sorry: *Imi pare rău*

Excuse me: *Pardon*

My name is John Smith: *Numele meu e John Smith*

Do you speak English?: *Vorbiţi engleză?*

Cheers!/Bless you!: *Noroc!*

How much is this?: *Cât costă (asta)?*

CHAPTER **FIVE**

ROMANIANS AT HOME

Lack of money, the high cost of travel, and family values have kept the home at the center of Romanian life. While the Communist-era buildings can be depressing, residents often put great effort into making their homes as pleasant as possible. It is not uncommon for extended families to live together, including grandparents who need care and adult children who cannot afford to move out.

A typical day starts with breakfast prepared by the mother, after which everyone heads off to school or work. Even the largest city, Bucharest, is relatively compact, so most people's journeys are far less than an hour, with the exception of people who travel between cities. In the past, many Romanians came home from work for lunch; now employees are more likely to have a bite in their office or stay in the vicinity of their workplace. Few take their full officially allowed lunch hour, not wanting to appear lazy in front of their boss or colleagues, even if they are only checking social media on their phone. Evenings are spent mostly at home watching TV, with younger people going out to a bar or restaurant.

Older women tend to spend the most time in the house, while their husbands meet other local men in a nearby pub or just on the street. Food trends are following those in the West: while in the past Romanians ate a lot of fresh food, sourced from their gardens or the local market, supermarkets and junk food have made inroads. Younger, more affluent city-dwellers also make use of grocery delivery apps like Bringo, and takeaway delivery apps like Bolt and Glovo, a trend that was given extra impetus by the pandemic-era lockdown.

HOUSE AND HOME

Romania's grim housing is one of the most visible legacies of the Communist regime. Monotonous, substandard, and dehumanizing, the notorious apartment complexes in which the majority of urban dwellers still live continue to scar the towns and cities, although there have been some efforts to paint over the gray in pastel colors over the last couple of decades. Inside the apartments, the utilities were poorly installed and are subject to regular suspensions and mishaps, and the weak walls do little to maintain privacy or keep out neighbors' noise. The inhabitants do not let the poor design and living conditions breed disrespect for their homes, however, and the areas in and around the complexes feel perfectly safe and not remotely intimidating, as they would in many Western cities. As well as keeping their own homes immaculate, many Romanians, particularly older women, decorate the communal hallways and stairwells with plants, and stick up pictures of prettier places and rural scenes.

Apartments were generally allocated by the Communists according to one's job, with people who worked in the same place often living in the same complex, and higher-ups (through party credentials rather than professional excellence) getting the pick of the better properties. Most apartments are on the small side for the number of people living in them, and sometimes the living room doubles as a bedroom for the parents. Adult children often live at home into their thirties and beyond. The noise level can be high, with clunking old elevators, loud music from other apartments, the old habit of beating of carpets outside (although this is less common among younger people as vacuum cleaners become more widespread), and neighbors' footsteps and DIY among the annoyances regularly endured by residents. Communism eroded privacy, and if you live in standard Romanian housing you may be subjected to visits from neighbors, who will often be well-intentioned and friendly.

Since the economic boom of the early and mid-2000s, there are also plenty of newbuild blocks in big cities, which are popular with young, affluent professionals, especially as many Romanians worry (with some justification) about the earthquake risks of older blocks. (Particularly vulnerable buildings may be marked with a red dot outside.)

If you are invited into a Romanian home, it is polite to remove your shoes—or at least to offer to—when you enter. The host will often have spare pairs of slippers for guests. Romanians seldom walk around barefoot, as they think by doing so one risks catching a cold, and will try to convince you to wear slippers too.

FOOD

Romanians—particularly the older ones—tend to be on the conservative side when it comes to food. Communist restrictions deprived the country of the opportunity to enjoy foreign foods and influences, and older people stick to a traditional diet of local, usually country, fare. Younger Romanians, with higher disposable income and more interest in the outside world, are more adventurous, and enjoy going to restaurants that serve foreign cuisines. The majority of such places are Italian—a culture with which Romanians feel comfortable and familiar—but more exotic cuisines are making inroads, at least in the big cities. Bucharest has a vibrant gastronomic scene that runs from fusion to sushi to vegan. These are no longer the preserve of international diners: as Romanians travel more and experience foreign food abroad, they are becoming more open to eating it in their homeland. That said, the local conservative palate typically shuns anything too spicy, and the international cuisine on offer may be far less piquant than the authentic version.

A traditional Moldavian dinner, including grilled meat and polenta.

Romanian cuisine is predominantly meat-based, with influences from the Balkans and Turkey. Pork is the most popular meat (some men joke that it is their favorite "vegetable"), followed by chicken and beef, then by fish and lamb, although the lamb eaten in Romania is typically quite tough. There's no real seafood culture, even on the coast (aside from the popular fried anchovies). Many vegetables are grown here, but they usually accompany the meaty main event rather than feature as meals in their own right, although there are a few honorable exceptions. Vegetarianism is unusual, veganism unheard of outside the big cities (if you shun meat it might be assumed you are unwell or have joined a cult). The exception is during "*post*"—or advent—periods before Easter and Christmas, when religious Romanians may give up meat.

Meals are typically hearty. They do not follow the "meat and two veg" model, and a "meal" may consist of just one or two constituent parts, like sausages, or sausages and fries or *mămăligă,* a polenta-like dish. At other times, however, meals will be substantial affairs, with soup, salad, meat, and drinks, all accompanied by a good dose of carbohydrates—bread, fries, or polenta. The Western concept of "healthy eating" is not yet well established in Romania, aside from among young and educated urbanites. Expect food and drink to be served with copious amounts of salt, sugar, oil, and fatty sauces. These are often added before they get to the table, denying you the chance to choose whether you want them or not.

Coffee culture has taken off hugely in the big cities. Cosmopolitan elites have largely ditched the Turkish-style coffee brewed in the traditional *ibric* (a small, long-handled metal pot) in favor of the Italian-style percolations of their Latin cousins, and these days it's hard to throw a coffee bean in central Bucharest without hitting a trendy café that sells top-quality cups of joe at—or even above—Western European prices. These venues typically provide free filtered tap water (in environmentally friendly glass bottles). This is a recent and limited phenomenon. Foreigners used to asking for a pitcher of tap water in restaurants back home would typically be met by bafflement when venturing such a request in a Romanian eatery: rusty pipes deter many Romanians from drinking the tap water, and waiters not only wouldn't want to serve impure water to their clients, they would find it odd that a customer would even ask for it.

Specialties

Although foreigners can find the local food uninspiring, there are several enjoyable delicacies. *Sarmale* are rolls of rice, vegetables, and minced meat wrapped in cabbage leaves; they are eaten in various forms throughout the Balkans. *Salatã de vinete* is roasted eggplant or eggplant salad with onions, a delightful dish that is great on toast, and one of the national cuisine's concessions to vegetarians. Opinion is divided on *mici,* mixed meat sausages that hold a similar place in Romanian culture to the beef burger elsewhere—these are often served up at outdoor celebrations, accompanied by beer. *Ciorbã de burtã*, or

Sarmale, here made of rice and mushrooms in a tomato sauce.

tripe soup, is something of an acquired taste, but several other soups are favorites among foreigners. Soups here tend not to be blended, as few people traditionally owned mixers and blenders, but are more in the style of broths.

Country Eating

On the back of globalization and modernization, supermarkets and hypermarkets have become well established, and even small towns and villages may be home to small supermarkets from international chains. The culture of markets and fresh food is still strong, however, particularly in the countryside. Many country households have enough land for some basic farming, growing tomatoes, cucumber, garlic, and onions, with some fruit trees and a few chickens. This means that if you get the chance to have a meal with a rural family, you're likely to enjoy fresh, organic produce that was picked a few moments earlier. For anyone used to lackluster supermarket produce, this is a real delight.

ALCOHOL

Alcohol is an integral part of Romanian life and culture. Traditional folk songs are often about getting together with friends and drinking until the sun comes up. Because the climate and soil are suited to viticulture, wine is cheap and plentiful, an effective way to unwind and forget the hard toil of rural life. In the countryside, the day's drinking can start as early as breakfast time. Wine's hold on rural communities is nothing new: the Dacian king Burebista is said to have ordered all the vines in the area torn up in the first century BCE to raise his people from their drunken torpor. Romanians traditionally prefer sweet wine; as a rule, the more expensive the establishment, the greater the share of dry varieties.

While urban dwellers might not start so early, alcohol remains an integral part of their lives. A dry celebration would be unthinkable. People are excluded from taking part in the many cheery toasts that punctuate a meal if they are on soft drinks, to the extent that a Romanian will visibly recoil rather than clink glasses with a nondrinker. The reason is superstition, but this, plus the pressure that teetotalers may come under to "join in," can create quite an oppressive atmosphere for anyone who doesn't want to drink.

On top of this, drink is easily accessible in terms of price, venues, and store hours. Alcohol is on sale in a far wider range of outlets than in the West, including gas stations, the cinema, and even some fast food joints like McDonald's and KFC. While imported brands are expensive, it is possible to buy local beer and spirits at low prices. There are no general restrictions on the sale of alcohol (aside from its being prohibited for those underage, and, surprisingly, near polling booths on election day), which can be bought twenty-four hours a day. Wine and beer are both popular, as is the traditional Romanian spirit *ţuică*, a kind of pungent plum brandy.

Despite the ubiquity of alcohol, it is quite rare to see obviously drunken Romanians on the street. Scenes you might come across in Northern and Western Europe, with young people strewn around the city center, fighting, vomiting, and slumped on the ground, are rare here. Perhaps the fear that people still have of authority makes them reluctant to indulge in unfettered self-expression and individuality. The legacy of the police state, where letting go and speaking freely could have serious consequences, could also be a factor.

Even rarer than a visibly drunk Romanian man is a visibly drunk Romanian woman. A double standard exists in that while it is generally accepted that getting drunk is something men do, an inebriated woman is more of a scandal. It has even been reported that scenes from the old television soap opera *Dallas*—tremendously popular in Romania in the 1980s—were edited to remove Sue Ellen's alcoholism, because women drinking was such a taboo.

HEALTH

Health is not a high priority for most Romanians, aside from the affluent Westernized class. Drinking and smoking rates are high, and a fatty, salty diet contributes to one of the lowest life expectancies in the EU (76.6 years in 2024 data). Given the tough times that people endured, it is easy to see why prolonging life became secondary to enjoying the moment with guilty pleasures. This was coupled with a general lack of health education, so that inaccurate knowledge was passed down the generations unchallenged. This is changing, though, as educated young professionals hit the gym and buy juicers, much like their counterparts elsewhere in the West.

The healthcare system has its problems. Previously struggling on pitifully low salaries, Romanian doctors once faced a stark choice: either abandon their local careers and head to the US, Canada, or Western Europe, supplement their meager income with bribes, or live with their parents and give up all hope of a better standard of living. Some do still emigrate for career advancement, but salaries have surged, and there are some excellent, well-trained, and committed medical staff working in Romania. Facilities in public hospitals may seem on the primitive side, but the treatment is perfectly adequate.

Foreigners may be surprised by the country's medical culture. Romanians are saturated by pharmacies and ads for treatments. They are quick to medicate: drugs are doled out for all kinds of minor ailments—a child's cough, or a cold, for example. Romania has one of the highest rates of antibiotic consumption rates in Europe, and they are often taken even when they are quite inappropriate for the malady being treated.

Romanians tend to be germophobic. As well as people taking off their shoes when entering their own or someone else's home, visitors to places like kindergartens and private clinics are also expected to wear shoe covers. As we have seen, Romanians fear that drafts and air-conditioning—

alongside going outside with wet hair—cause a variety of maladies, and will worry for you if you expose yourself to these threats.

TELEVISION

At the center of Romanian home life is the television set. In some households it is on almost continuously from the time of the first member waking up to the last person going to bed. People rely on the TV for news as well as entertainment, although it now has a formidable rival in the cell phone, which even older Romanians have embraced.

TV established a stranglehold on Romanian life for both political and financial reasons. Under Communism, programming consisted mainly of two hours a day of dreary propaganda supplemented by the odd Soviet movie. When independent companies introduced new, international shows in the 1990s, the public was thrilled, and watching TV became an enjoyable way to throw off the past. Low incomes previously put the cinema, opera, or restaurant beyond the means of many people. TV, on the other hand, was free entertainment.

This huge enthusiasm for TV has not always been matched by quality. One of the staples is the *telenovela*, a melodramatic type of soap opera imported from South America. Turkish ones have become popular, and Romania now has homegrown versions too. Local copies of foreign cookery shows such as *MasterChef*, and talent contests (for example, *Romania's Got Talent* and *Dancing with the Stars*) also attract large audiences. Variety shows and anything reuniting estranged families are popular with older and less educated viewers. Local programs were often characterized by low production values, an overload of sentiment, and a sexist presentation of women, although this is changing with acclaimed output such as the 2023 HBO thriller *Spy/Master*, a Romanian co-production partly filmed in the country (in parallel with the acclaimed work of movie directors such as Cristian Mungiu, Corneliu Porumboiu, and Radu Jude).

In any case, most Romanians have a cable TV package and get a full range of international channels such as the BBC, CNN, National Geographic, Animal Planet, and MTV, while younger and higher-earning viewers have embraced streaming platforms like Netflix, HBO, Disney Plus, and so on.

THE FAMILY

The family is an important social unit, and Romanians typically have strong family ties. Many adult children still live at home, and while this is due in part to unaffordable housing, Romanian mothers often do little to encourage their offspring to leave the nest, providing a full service of cooked meals and all laundry done. Far from seeming anxious to have their own place, many Romanians in their twenties and thirties—particularly men—are quite happy to stay at home and be catered to. Interdependence usually takes precedence over independence in Romanian families. Grandparents, particularly widowed or ailing ones, also commonly live with one of their children's families.

These family bonds keep people in close proximity to one another. While many young Romanians do go abroad, either for a better salary or to further their career, plenty who are interested in the outside world reject the idea because it would mean being a long way from siblings and parents. While some young people move from their hometown—usually to a bigger city to work or study—they still retain strong links with their parents, returning for regular weekend visits, often with dirty laundry in tow.

CHILDREN

Romania has a very child-friendly culture. If you're with a young baby, complete strangers may say "*să vă trăiască*," a form of congratulations. Children are typically more indulged than in the West, which can be irritating if you're in a restaurant and screaming children are running around unchecked by their seemingly oblivious parents (although this is less common since the advent of smartphones). The flip side of this is that you need not worry about feeling like a pariah if your own young ones start acting up. Boys are especially indulged, with boisterousness considered par for the course. This child-friendliness is often more evident in attitude than in actual facilities, however, as many restaurants lack high chairs and children's menus, although this is starting to improve. There are many public playgrounds, and while some can be rickety and run-down, others, especially in large cities, are well equipped and great fun for kids, as well as an opportunity for socializing among parents. Many Romanians are not shy about involving themselves in other families' child-rearing, and while the unsolicited (and often ill-founded) advice you'll receive from strangers may be irksome, if your child is lost, hurt, upset, or bullied outside of your eyeshot, well-meaning bystanders will usually try to help.

Because of the Ceaușescu government's policies, which encouraged mothers to return to work and leave their children in daycare, some women today go straight back to work soon after giving birth, despite employees being entitled to up to two years' paid leave (which many more affluent mothers take). On weekdays, parks are full of grandparents pushing prams (and Filipina nannies in upmarket areas). Gender socialization starts early. Baby girls are decked out in pink and usually have their ears pierced so strangers know they are female. As elsewhere, educated and professional women tend to have children later in life than uneducated ones; overall, though, the age at which women give birth to their first child is among the lowest in the EU: 27.1 years in 2024.

Adults typically don't like children in their care to get dirty or sweaty, or to splash around in puddles, even in places like parks, as they think it will make them ill. Romanian parents tend to overdress their infants, and it's

Two sisters celebrating *Ziua Iei*, or the International Day of the Romanian Blouse, Constanta.

common to see children swathed in blankets or in hats and thick coats even when it's not especially cold. You can expect frequent admonishments from strangers if your offspring are sockless indoors or hatless on a mild afternoon.

EDUCATION

Romanian schooling comes in four main stages: optional kindergarten (*grădiniță*, or *învățământul preșcolar*); elementary school (*școala primară*) for grades zero to four and gymnasium (*gimnaziu*) for grades five to eight; high school (*liceu*) for grades nine to twelve; and higher education (*studii superioare*). Children start school at the age of six, and attendance is compulsory until the age of sixteen. High schools may be based on the liberal arts or technical in nature. Private schools represent a small percentage of the total and cater largely to expatriate children and the offspring of rich Romanians. The public system has been somewhat resistant to modernization, and attracts criticism from some parents for the outdated syllabi, learning by rote, and academic pressure heaped on students—although other parents approve of this rigorous approach, and believe pupils learn more than in Western European schools. Children are given significant homework from a young age, although many do it at their after-school—establishments set up to cater for children outside the short official school day. There are too few classrooms for pupils, so schools are taught in shifts: classes may begin as early as 7:30 a.m. or as late as 1:00 p.m. Many families opt for private tutoring (*meditații*) to improve their children's chances of getting into a good school or university. Romanians often maintain friendships with classmates, particularly as many tend to remain living in the same area.

A COUPLE-CENTRIC SOCIETY

In the street, in the park, in the restaurant, in the supermarket—couples are everywhere in Romania. It is assumed that everyone must be looking for a mate, and single people, especially women, may be the objects of some pity or even clumsy attempts at matchmaking in more traditional communities. Couples are expected to do most things as a unit, and too much independence or a separate social life can be read by others as a sign of something wrong in the relationship. It is expected that when someone is in a relationship, the time spent socializing with their friends will be cut down, and this is not considered a reason to take offense.

MARRIAGE

Although, as throughout Europe, cohabiting is an increasingly popular choice, marriage remains the gold standard in religious, traditional Romania (the fact that independent liberal candidate Nicușor Dan was not married to his long-term partner and mother of his children was used against him in the 2025 presidential election campaign). Parents still hope for their children to get married, after a period of living together, and may frequently tell them so. Women are, on average, 28.3 at the age of their first marriage, men 31.5. These figures have risen steadily. Independence and privacy within marriage are not universally accepted concepts—some spouses may keep tabs on each other, calling and messaging many times a day and checking each other's cell phones, while opposite-sex friendships may be viewed with suspicion outside cosmopolitan circles. Divorce remains low by European levels, probably due to the country's strong religious morality and women's still more limited economic opportunities. After divorce, lack of money forces some couples to stay living in the same house.

LOVE AND SEXUALITY

Sexuality runs through the entirety of Romanian society. Perhaps due to Latin sensuality, perhaps as a reaction to the fall of Communism, perhaps because their society is still trying to work out its values, sex can seem all around you in Romania. Passionate kissing and caressing are common in public, particularly in parks, which play host to lovers still living with their parents. Some advertisers have yet to move beyond simply associating their products with a cleavage-baring woman. Some women still dress in a surprisingly provocative way to Western visitors—even news anchors and businesswomen may appear in low-cut tops, skirts that look more like belts, and heavy, obvious makeup (although the trend is much less marked than it used to be, as local sartorial mores shift toward Western standards).

But while the style of dress favored by some women would suggest that Romanians are a liberated, sexually confident people, this is not typically the case. Romania is a conservative country where religion still informs attitudes, and there is a fixed and narrow idea of what constitutes appropriate sexual behavior. Under Communism any discussion of sex was taboo—aghast parents rushed to protect their children from the mildest sexual content on TV, which was in any event vigorously censored—and as a result the younger generation grew up viewing sex as something shrouded in shame. This is now changing, with cosmopolitan Millennials and Gen Z being much more open and relaxed about sexual matters, which they discuss with less inhibition.

Despite increasing Westernization, prejudices persist. Many Romanians, including even some young and educated people, are still stridently homophobic: in 2025, Romania overtook Poland as the worst country in the EU for LGBTQ people, according to Brussels-based NGO ILGA-Europe. Bucharest does have a few venues for gay people, but the scene is nascent and an openly gay couple would be at risk of some hostility, or at least glares, in public. Gay pride parades, which have taken place annually since 2005, were initially met with dramatic denunciations and protest marches by right-wing and religious groups, and even some physical attacks on participants. Opposition, however, has now largely shrunk to a few defiant church bells ringing and some mocking and jibes from passersby and the media, while the march itself goes from strength to strength—a sign of the steady, albeit slow, progress. A 2018 attempt to change the Romanian Constitution to define marriage as between a man and woman—and thereby specifically ban same-sex unions—failed due to low turnout.

This highlights something that Westerners may perceive as an inconsistency in Romanian sexual mores, that deviating from the gold-standard heterosexual marriage can be judged more harshly than exploitative and abusive sexual behavior. Many would consider heterosexual adultery, for example—or at least a married man having a mistress, which is held up as a status symbol by some—as more understandable and acceptable than a loving and equal gay partnership.

Dating apps such as Tinder are well used in the cities, though some users warn of scams: escorts use the sites with undeclared financial motives, and foreign men may be more at risk of being targeted due to their perceived wealth. These platforms are particularly useful for LGBTQ individuals, who could face stigma in offline dating attempts, although the communities are fairly small.

Attitudes to selling sex are relatively lax. Prostitution itself was decriminalized in 2014, though some of the associated activities remain criminal offences. Many people still regard it as a legitimate outlet for men, with little thought for the welfare of the women. As elsewhere, the industry is less visible now—you're unlikely to still find flyers for prostitutes around the entrances to upmarket-looking restaurants—as it has moved online. Foreign men may be at particular risk of being robbed by prostitutes and pimps.

Pedophilia is not discussed much, but the poverty and disastrous child policies of the past Communist regime left a legacy of vulnerable young people, and this coupled with an inefficient legal system led to foreign criminals targeting Romania's street children and other youngsters. Fortunately, with European integration, child welfare has become more of a priority.

CHAPTER SIX

TIME OUT

Romanians embrace their leisure time with gusto. With a harsh past and an uncertain future, they throw themselves into the present and live it up. Higher salaries and proliferating restaurants, bars, and new American-style entertainment options have opened up a plethora of new ways to pass the time away from the TV set. Alcohol often helps things along. Romanians are legally entitled to twenty days' leave from work, in addition to around fifteen days of statutory holiday, but ambitious professionals often don't take the full entitlement. It's possible to pay for most things by card or contactless cell phone payment these days, with the occasional exception in small villages and businesses.

ROMANIANS RELAXING

In contrast to Communist times, where provided one clocked in at work one could often be home again within a few hours without anyone complaining, today's Romanians work long and hard hours. As a result, they like to make the most of their leisure time: weekends, from Friday evening to Sunday night, and public holidays are much looked forward to. Traditionally, a great deal of leisure activity involved going out in sets of couples—it was rare to see groups of female friends on a girls' night out, although young men socialized together a bit more. The disparity was even more pronounced among older Romanians: while men gathered to drink and, before the ban, smoke in small, basic bars known as *birt-uri*, more mature women seldom met for coffee or lunch (apart from breaks with work colleagues). But rising incomes and the erosion of such rigid gender norms are changing this. Many men are keen gamblers, going to casinos and betting on far-flung foreign football teams they know nothing of, and slot machine arcades are a thriving area of business—you won't walk far in a Romanian town without coming across a betting shop. As elsewhere, though, much of the trade has moved online.

Romanians tend to socialize in conventional ways. Popular venues are bars, restaurants (often for special occasions), parks, and malls. Bowling, pool, and the cinema are also popular among the young, while escape rooms have also taken off in cities over the last decade or so. Most leisure activities are accessible to foreigners, as members of staff often speak some English.

There are museums and galleries, particularly in Bucharest and the larger cities. More highbrow diversions, such as ballet, classical music, and opera are all available for bargain ticket prices.

Popular weekend activities for locals include trips to the mountains—and the beach in the summer—and family picnics or grills in nearby green areas.

Young Romanians eagerly adopt international trends, and consequently now spend a lot of their leisure time online; older people too are often keen cell phone converts. Facebook and WhatsApp are the most popular platforms, while Instagram and TikTok have also gained traction, especially with younger users, some of whom "hang out" with each other virtually. Teens do still enjoy real-life contact, though screens feature heavily, as with Gen Z elsewhere in the world.

RESTAURANTS

After the scarcity and limited range of food under Communism, restaurants soon became a popular novelty. The dominant fare is local cuisine, or Italian. International foods are now also well established, in the big cities, at least, with young diners especially experimenting with exotic new tastes. The days when expatriates bemoaned the lack of decent Asian food in the country, complaining that if you wanted anything non-European you'd be hard pressed to find it, are mostly gone. This is largely because of younger Romanians' increased access to foreign travel, and in the capital and other major cities restaurants serving a wealth of different cuisines (*specifice*) are springing up all the time, although the trend is likely to take longer to permeate the rest of the country.

Some diners like to research restaurants online, on Trip Advisor or Restograf.ro. While many eateries come and go, there are several stalwarts in the major towns whose reputations are well deserved.

Local restaurant etiquette may be less formal and louder than foreigners are used to. Some places pack in tables to maximize revenue, and you may find your relaxing meal marred by people whose unashamedly booming voices raise the general sound level. Employees may play loud music of their own choice that is inappropriate to the restaurant—thumping house music

Large outdoor seating area for eating and drinks, Bucharest.

to accompany Sunday lunch in a beautifully decorated eatery, for example. Few Romanians consider phones ringing loudly and being answered during a meal to be rude.

Children are routinely brought into restaurants, even at late hours. While the local tendency to indulge rather than discipline unruly offspring previously saw kids running around unchecked by parents, this is less of an irritation now that children, even toddlers, are kept quiescent by smartphones.

Customer service can be hit and miss. Many people worked for the state under Communism, and they retained their jobs through connections, not productivity. Nobody cared if their employer made money or not, and there was no incentive to work hard or well. This mentality has unfortunately been passed on, and it is possible, even in the more upmarket restaurants, to struggle vainly to catch the attention of chatting staff, or to be served by surly or inept individuals. But this is improving, especially as young Romanians work in the service industry in Western Europe for a few years, then return home with a new concept of what constitutes good service.

While prices are rising, eating out in Romania can still be good value. Expect an informal, fun environment rather than a sophisticated evening out, and have patience with the minor irritations, and you can enjoy some great food in a lively atmosphere. Among the top restaurants, the service, style, and cuisine are as good as any in the West. Romanians usually like to divide the bill according to what they have consumed rather than split it equally—the many people still on low salaries can rarely afford to be liberal with their money.

Some foreigners get embarrassed by the discourteous way in which certain Romanians—often the nouveau riche—address waitstaff. In a transition society where people may be insecure about their status, some individuals have felt they could assert their position by speaking down to those they considered to be beneath them, such as workers in the service industry. This behavior is fortunately becoming much less common.

In Romania, the term "restaurant" also extends to fast food outlets, which are incredibly popular. This is partly due to enthusiasm for all things American, but also because such eateries came as a welcome change after decades of the homogeneous Communist-era diet. Romanians still seize upon anything new from the West with fervor. Another advantage that fast food businesses have had is that their standards of service, consistency, and hygiene compare favorably with other cheap eateries. With the health message slowly getting through and the novelty wearing off, however, the initial eagerness is now waning a little—but McDonald's and KFC still do a roaring trade.

CLUBS AND BARS

Romanians started celebrating after the revolution in 1989, and (pandemic notwithstanding) do not seem to have

TIPPING

Waiters have tended to expect lower tips than is common elsewhere in Europe. Rounding up the bill or leaving slightly below 10 percent has been the norm. Some Romanians tell the waiter how much to take by way of a tip when the payment for the meal is collected. Foreign visitors can find this awkward, and it is perfectly fine to leave the tip on the table when you go. When paying by card or phone, some handheld payment devices give the option to add a percentage-based gratuity.

In a taxi, rounding up the fare is appreciated. If you pay with a higher-value note, some drivers will hand you your change grudgingly, if at all, although the situation is getting better, particularly with the advent of apps like Uber, Bolt, and Star Taxi, where passengers can leave feedback on drivers. Other professionals who appreciate a tip include hairdressers and beauticians, but some Romanians leave their change for all manner of poorly paid employees, from hospital staff and postal workers to shop assistants.

When tipping in general, rounding up the bill is usually considered sufficient, unless it comes to a very small sum or the service was exceptional. In better restaurants and more international venues you may wish to leave around 15 percent.

stopped since. Nightclubs can be packed (sometimes to the point of enforced immobility) and lively, with a sizable percentage of the crowd still going strong at closing time, which can be as late as 5:00 a.m. Many people dance for most of the night, and although a lot of alcohol is consumed, the atmosphere is generally a happy one, unsullied by drunkenness or violence. Prior to the smoking ban, clubs could be incredibly fumy, and the health and safety aspects also left a lot to be desired, although many of the more dangerous venues closed down or embarked upon renovation following the fatal fire at Colectiv in October 2015. In general, though, they are spirited places and can be a lot of fun.

Bathroom Etiquette

A few quirks of bathroom etiquette may come as a surprise to the first-time visitor. If it is unclear whether a cubicle is occupied (locks are often old-fashioned bolts and seldom have a red indicator or "occupied" sign), a person waiting will knock on the door. This is considered a practical necessity, not an intrusion. Clearly any reply you give will suffice to convey your presence, but the usual response is "*ocupat*," meaning "occupied."

Another thing to be aware of is that some Romanian women stand, rather than sit, on the toilet seat in public conveniences, and assume a crouching position similar to that required for a squat toilet (very rare in Romania, and almost nonexistent in major cities). This perilous maneuver is prompted by their fear that the seat is dirty. The result is that a nightclub toilet seat, say, can be covered in grimy footprints, rendering it unusable. Fortunately, the practice is quite rare and you won't find it in upmarket places.

Romanians can be very strict about gender-specific bathroom use: in public places like malls, even quite young boys are typically expected to use the men's bathroom, rather than the women's bathroom with their mothers, and fellow users of the facilities will not be shy about sharing their views on this. Counterarguments about the safety of unaccompanied children carry little weight. Given many restroom patrons' aversion to the sight of even a five-year-old boy in the ladies' room, perhaps it is a relief that the trans bathroom debate seems light years from reaching Romania.

Many venues, particularly basement clubs, are cheap and unpretentious, but Bucharest has a few self-consciously trendy superclubs that fly in top international DJs. These are the places where the city's poseurs *(fițoși)* go to see and be seen—you are expected to look the part. The scene has diversified, with some venues hosting events such as standup comedy, pub quizzes, board game evenings, karaoke, and jam nights, alongside the more traditional live music. Unlike in some Western countries, Romanian nightlife seems not to have dropped off post-pandemic, with some venues having even managed to continue hosting furtive parties during lockdown.

Bars vary from basic, men-only (in practice, if not officially) canteens selling cheap draft beer, wine, and spirits to plush international-style cocktail lounges, where the prices differ little from Western capitals. Romania has fairly liberal licensing laws: if you want to keep drinking all night long, you can usually find a place to do it, at least if you're in a larger city. There is no tradition of buying rounds; people order what they want—the vast majority of places have table service—and the bill comes at the end of the night when, unless someone is playing host and therefore paying, it is divided according to individual consumption.

AT THE MALL

Representing consumerism, wealth, and the West—everything people were denied access to by the Communists—malls are beloved by Romanians. If you refer to a shopping center that existed prior to 1989 as a mall, you will be corrected, even if nobody can point out the difference. Romanians are adamant that the mall "concept" is a modern one. Many people get dressed up to go to the mall—it is taken seriously. Buying things is only a small part of the visit; it's more about the experience and, for some, the social cachet. Mall food courts are almost constantly packed. Most malls have entertainment in the form of amusement arcades, bowling alleys, and cinemas. Some have even branched out into ice rinks and soft play areas.

THE CINEMA

Although the situation is much better than it used to be, talkers can sometimes blight the cinema experience in Romania. While the vast majority of spectators sit quietly, complete audience silence is not guaranteed outside the most highbrow or tragic films, or small audiences. Cell phones ring—and are answered. A shush sometimes shames a talkative viewer into silence.

On the positive side, foreign features in Romania are subtitled, not dubbed. Most movies reach Romania fairly soon after, or concurrently with, their release in Western cinemas. Prices are low in comparison to other European countries, although tickets at mall multiplexes may be only slightly lower than the cheapest cinemas elsewhere. While they are being edged out by the multiplexes, non-mall movie theaters run from the plush and modern to the delightfully archaic, often state-funded venues charging rock-bottom rates and showing an impressive range of pictures, from ninety-year-old German silent films to Hollywood classics and offbeat indie flicks. Film festivals on everything from feminism to Dracula take place regularly; the flagship one is the Transilvania International Film Festival, which has been going for nearly a quarter of a century.

THEATER, OPERA, CONCERTS, AND JAZZ

If you're not expecting the variety and tradition of London or Paris, Bucharest enjoys a flourishing arts scene. While most plays may be of limited interest to non-Romanian speakers, there is the odd performance in English, or occasionally with surtitles above the stage. Consult websites and social media to see what's on. Even the most expensive ticket would be unlikely to set you back more than US $50; they are often much cheaper. Stadium concerts by visiting stars, which are now fairly common in the capital and major cities, music festivals, and local versions of Broadway-style shows cost more, but are still cheaper than in the West. Jazz fans are also well catered to, with regular gigs showcasing traditional and more experimental music. Jam sessions have also sprung up in the big cities over the past decade or so.

Drama, classical, jazz, and other artistic fields are all celebrated in a remarkable array of festivals—many outdoor and free—of which the most high-profile is the biennial George Enescu Festival, named for the classical composer. Various other al fresco performances are also held in the warmer months.

The main arts venues are equally impressive. The National Theater is an imposing, modern-looking monolith built by a group of local architects. Located in the middle of Bucharest, it hosts exhibitions and tours of the building as well as the country's top drama. The venue reopened in 2015 after extensive renovation. The Opera (it is never called the Opera House) is a plush, opulent auditorium, completed by socialist-realist designer Octav Doicescu in 1953, which recalls

The Romanian Athenaeum, Bucharest.

the capital's bygone glory days. Classical concerts are also staged at the neoclassical Athenaeum, possibly the country's most beautiful building, and Sala Radio in Bucharest, as well as in regional venues.

PARKS

On a warm weekend or public holiday, the main parks and gardens are packed with playing children, cavorting couples, and groups of elderly friends watching the world go by. There are boating lakes, cafés and bars, children's playgrounds—in short, something for everyone. Less crowded parks host informal football matches, and their pathways a hybrid game of soccer-tennis. They are extremely well tended, and in spring come alive with planted floral displays. The best thing about parks in Romania is that they are often populated until late at night, with families lingering in playgrounds, couples out for a midnight stroll, and drinkers finishing up at the cafés; and they also have security guards, so they do not become the preserve of gangs and drug dealers, as can happen elsewhere.

Previously, in smaller parks nobody was allowed on the grass, and venturing onto it could have got you scolded—possibly even fined—if a guard saw you. However, the authorities had a change of heart over this, and friendly signs are sometimes erected inviting parkgoers onto the grass in many (though not all) green spaces.

SPORTS AND PASTIMES

For Romanians, sports are usually about watching rather than participating. Soccer is passionately supported, and rivalry matchups involving any of the five major clubs—Bucharest-based Rapid, FCSB (formerly Steaua), and Dinamo, alongside Universitatea Craiova and CFR Cluj—engender strong emotions, as do the national team's matches against other countries.

Such vociferous support has largely been undeserved—and unrewarded. Despite having some talented players, Romanian soccer was held back for many years by corruption, the poor lifestyle habits of some players, and lack of professionalism among agents and the people in charge of the game, many of whom were dubious "businessmen" with little knowledge of the game, who routinely sacked coaches on a whim. The result of this was years of underachievement. Football fans like to hark back to when the national side beat England in Euro 2000, and Steaua's European Cup victory in 1986. However, wider societal advancements and the imprisonment of some big-name moguls in the 2010s have helped clean the sport up somewhat.

Watching soccer in Romania can be enjoyable—there's always a lively atmosphere, and some of the comments shouted at the players can be amusing, if profane. The swanky national arena (*Arena Națională*), which opened in 2011, hosted UEFA Euro 2020 matches (in 2021), and the big clubs are gradually occupying new or improved stadia. Tickets are still quite cheap, though prices leap when major international teams visit.

On mainstream TV, coverage is routinely interrupted by quick commercials, and ads are beamed onto the screen from time to time, which can be annoying for fans unused to it. However, online streaming options and dedicated sports channels like Digi Sport and Prima Sport have improved the viewing experience.

With Western health and fitness messages slowly permeating the country, there is a growing number of gyms (which Romanians refer to as "fitness") offering equipment, personal training, group classes from Aqua to Zumba, and sometimes massages and saunas. Gymgoers are often businesspeople or white-collar professionals. You can also find facilities for tennis and five-a-side soccer. The influx of foreign investment and accompanying businessmen after Communism started a wave of golf course development: the number has reached low double figures and is steadily rising, with a few 18-hole options.

On the more cerebral side, checkers and chess are hugely popular, probably due to the Communist encouragement of chess (Lenin called it the "gymnasium of the mind"). You often find impromptu games on the street, and semi-organized meets—exclusively involving old men—in places like Cismigiu Park in Bucharest.

VACATIONS

Because foreign travel has only become a realistic prospect for most people in the last couple of decades, vacations were generally limited to domestic destinations—either the seaside or the mountains. (There is also the Danube Delta, but high prices and undeveloped tourist facilities have held that area back.) When one can and cannot go also seems to be fairly regimented: Romanians talk of the first or last suitable weekend of the season for going to the seaside (a weather-based assessment, with the assumption that nobody would think of going to a beach when it is cold).

Both areas have much in their favor. The Black Sea beaches are sandy, and the sea temperature is usually warm enough for a dip in season; but while some tourist resorts have improved with investment, others still lack decent infrastructure and have a tacky feel, while the beaches can suffer from litter. The resorts are also relatively expensive; many Romanians find it cheaper or better value to go to Bulgaria or Greece. The mountain areas offer fine scenery, hiking, and skiing opportunities, but can also suffer from high prices and poor service, though again, standards are improving. Despite the drawbacks, the Romanian fun-loving spirit usually triumphs, with people flocking to the resorts and having a fine time there. As incomes have increased, more affluent Romanians have started to enjoy mini-breaks in Western European cities, and

Ski slope in Poiana Brasov.

packages to Egypt and even further afield are advertised in most travel agency windows and online.

DRESS CODES

In the wake of Communism, fashion trends spread through the country, particularly among the urban populace, and there has been a certain homogeneity in how people dress, with more adventurous youngsters sporting punk or goth attire prompting raised eyebrows—although greater diversity of style is now becoming more common in the big cities. Many young Romanians have adopted the standard Western dress code of jeans and sneakers.

Until fairly recently, some Romanian women dressed in a sexually provocative way that astonished foreign visitors. This was not limited to nights out; it was not unheard of to see women teetering around the supermarket in heels and a miniskirt on a Monday morning, reflecting the huge emphasis placed on a woman's physical appearance and the thinking that her priority should be to look "sexy." This was also partly a reaction to the Communist period, when decent cosmetics and clothing were not readily available. Clothes came in standard, drab colors and styles, and any individuality would require the work of a tailor—although too much would have been frowned on. This sort of skimpy getup is much less common in the larger cities as Western norms come to dominate the local sartorial scene, while lockdown-era home working reduced high-heeled office power dressing. While some rural women still glam themselves up, others adopt casual attire more suited to the rigors of village life.

Menswear is also closely aligned to Western norms, with jeans, sneakers, and T-shirts popular for casual occasions, and business suits for work—although many offices permit more relaxed attire. Subgroups such as the Roma have a more distinctive style—rather than looking to the West for tips, they look to the East, and much of their clothing has a Turkish flavor. Some of the women still wear long, colorful peasant skirts.

If you're going out for a special occasion, it's typical to make an effort with your appearance, although foreigners' idiosyncrasies are tolerated, and if you turn up looking casual bordering on scruffy, it is unlikely that anyone will mind much. An exception to the dress-up rule is funerals, which mourners typically attend in their day-to-day clothes.

25
CFR PROGRESUL
DEPOUL MILITARI
STB
184

CHAPTER **SEVEN**

TRAVEL, HEALTH, & SAFETY

Thanks mainly to EU funds, Romania's network of previously potholed regional roads is much improved. Although construction is perennially beset by delays, contract squabbles, and quality issues, the total coverage of highways of a decent standard is constantly growing, bringing journey times around Romania down.

Public transportation often brings you into close contact with local people. In some cases, such as sociable long-distance train journeys, where family photos, opinions, and snacks are shared around the car, this can be a pleasant distraction. In other instances, like being squashed sardine style into a jam-packed Bucharest bus, missing your stop because there's no prospect of reaching the door, it is less welcome. Nevertheless, the good thing is that travel in Romania largely remains one of the country's true bargains.

ARRIVAL

Most foreign visitors will fly into Bucharest's Otopeni Airport. In 2004 its name was changed to Henri Coanda International Airport, after the Romanian flight pioneer, but this fact seems to have passed most people by, and it is still nearly universally referred to as Otopeni.

In 2012, a spanking new departures terminal was opened (in a bid to deal with congestion), finally giving Bucharest an airport worthy of an EU capital—right down to the extortionately priced sandwiches! This was the latest phase in an impressive transformation that sought to spruce up the airport itself and rid it of the stains on its reputation, such as the phalanx of unofficial taxi drivers waiting for a gullible foreigner to transport to the city center for about ten times the correct fare. Today an automated touchscreen system allows newly landed passengers to order a cab from a legitimate Bucharest taxi firm or a ride-share. The odd hopeful crook remains from the bad old days, so ignore any approaches in the terminal and head straight for the touchscreens.

An alternative, cheaper means of getting between town and the airport is the 100 bus, which leaves from outside the domestic terminal. A rechargeable Activ card, which you can subsequently use on other public transport, can be bought from a machine or the kiosk at the bus stop (if open) and scanned on board; you can also simply scan a payment card or phone or send an SMS. A train also serves the airport, but only leaves once every forty minutes—although given the infernal Bucharest traffic, it may still be the quickest option during rush hour. A metro link to the airport is planned.

A second airport, Aurel Vlaicu International Airport, known as Băneasa Airport from the neighborhood where it is located—in between the main airport and the city center—also serves Bucharest.

These days, the expansion of cheap flight networks throughout Eastern Europe means that numerous routes serve other Romanian cities too, so if your final destination is not Bucharest you may be able to fly in directly.

WALKING

Even the largest city in Romania, Bucharest, has a small center, relatively easy to traverse on foot. Many of Romania's prettiest places are unpublicized, and walking is a great way to discover delightful streets, gardens, and buildings. One of the main barriers to a pleasant stroll is the state of the sidewalks. While the authorities are slowly getting around to repairing the road network and sidewalks, some of the latter remain neglected, with holes and bumps. Even decent sidewalks in the city are often blocked by cars parked directly across them, forcing pedestrians into the road—where motorists then honk their horns at them—although this is gradually improving, at least in central areas.

BICYCLES AND SCOOTERS

With its heavy traffic and cavalier approach to road safety, Bucharest has not traditionally been a cyclist-friendly city. Efforts have been made to address this, with cycle lanes patchily implemented along some of the main arteries and bike hire schemes popping up here and there, albeit with little longevity. The electric scooter, offered for hire to Bucharest residents by the likes of Bolt and Lyme, has had more success, perhaps in part because of the ease of leaving it anywhere, rather than having to return it to a docking point. In smaller towns and villages, bikes are popular as a cheaper way to cover shorter distances.

Rental bikes in Piatra Neamț.

BUSES AND STREETCARS

Buses and streetcars (known in Romania as trams) are the main form of public transportation in the larger cities. In Bucharest the system is comprehensive and often quick, although of course it is subject to the vicissitudes of the traffic. You rarely have to wait long during the day; night services are less frequent. Ticketing is now fully electronic through the Activ card, which is on sale at certain marked kiosks at major interchanges, and can be topped up at the smaller kiosks found by some bus and streetcar stops until around 8:30 or 9:00 p.m. on weekdays and early afternoon on Saturdays (and sometimes Sundays). It must be scanned on board. The Multiplu card, which comes with a set number of journeys and cannot then be topped up, is a good option for shorter stays. Daily, weekly, monthly, and annual passes are available. You can also pay for ninety minutes of bus and streetcar travel by scanning your bank card or cell phone (if it has contactless payment enabled), via SMS from a Romanian-registered cell phone or with the 24Pay mobile app. Other large cities employ similar systems.

The flip side of their cheapness, frequency, and relative efficiency is that Bucharest buses and streetcars can become uncomfortably packed, to the extent that the doors are barely able to close and faces and bodies are pressed up against the glass. The fleet is being renewed, and many of the new buses and streetcars are modern and sophisticated, with air-conditioning and comfortable upholstered seating. The crowded conditions have traditionally made public transportation fertile territory for pickpockets. However, thieves have become far fewer in recent years, with many locals bitterly joking that this is because following EU accession, the country's pickpockets have chosen to apply their skills in Western Europe.

THE METRO

Bucharest's underground train system, known as the metro, with its more predictable journey times, is often the best way to cover long distances, especially in rush hour. The only logistical downside is that the network is not as comprehensive. The city has practically finished renewing its subway fleet, which means that the old graffiti-covered cars that looked like something out of 1980s New York have largely given way to sleek and pristine new trains.

Foreign visitors will find a few frustrations when traveling by metro. At busy stations, in their haste to get on, the waiting passengers sometimes crowd around the door when the train arrives, thereby allowing only one person to disembark at a time, rather than the three who would be able to do so if the doorway were left clear. This slows things down somewhat. Escalator use can be another annoyance for anyone in a hurry—the authorities' valiant efforts to establish the "stand on

The Obor station in the Bucharest Metro.

the right" principle of, say, the London Underground, through repeated public campaigns seem to have petered out, and passengers position themselves on the left or right as their whim dictates, making it hard for others to walk up or down.

TRAINS

Long-distance trains come in three categories: Regio, Interregio, and Intercity. Regio services (formerly known as *personal*), the slowest and cheapest, make frequent stops in the remotest of outposts. They should only be considered if funds are tight or if you are looking for an interesting cultural experience. (They do tend to carry the chattiest passengers, probably because the journeys are so long, they need to do something to pass the time.) At the other end of the scale, most intercity trains, while still relatively good value, offer either old-school charm or sleek modernity, with the first-class compartments rivaling the best for comfort and service. If you're traveling abroad or over a long distance in Romania, sleeper cars can be a good option, although there can be a difference in service and attitude on trains heading west of Romania and trains heading east, north, or south. Whatever train you're on, the one thing that might be missing is a decent café car, so it is worth taking your own provisions.

TAXIS

Although taxi fares have soared in recent years, they are still much lower than in Western countries. Taxis can be booked by app (or phone, though this is less typical now), or hailed in the street; the latter should be avoided unless you are in a desperate rush, as you will almost certainly be massively overcharged. (If you find yourself in this predicament, at least make sure you establish the fare at the start of the journey.) Most drivers will activate their meter automatically, but if they don't it's better to request it than to get into an argument at your destination.

Uber, Bolt, and others operate in an expanding network of larger towns and cities. Romanian cab drivers in general, and Bucharest ones in particular, once had something of a reputation for lying, cheating, bigoted small talk, taking circuitous routes, smoking, and driving recklessly. The advent of the Star Taxi app with driver feedback and ratings, combined with competition from ride-sharing apps, has hugely improved the situation, though foreigners especially should still keep their wits about them. Unsolicited offers of a taxi should be firmly declined. As we've seen, it is usual to give a small tip at the journey's end.

DRIVING

Although it has improved significantly in recent years, navigating Romania's road system can be a chaotic, dangerous, illogical nightmare. The frequent honking, lack of respect for pedestrians, and counterproductive blocking of the way are unfathomable and frustrating. Bucharest sees the worst of it. Some motorists are aggressive and impatient, honking a second or two after the lights change if the car in front does not immediately move. Some will even sound the horn if it is obvious that the road is blocked and nobody can go anywhere. As soon as one horn sounds, several other drivers may join in, as if not to do so would be proof of weakness. Drivers often block intersections in the hope of making the light, rather than wait for the way to clear, even though this clearly brings no benefit and holds up other lanes of traffic.

Pedestrians have it worst. The yellow light sometimes allows drivers to proceed if a pedestrian crossing is clear. In practice this means that while you cross, cars will edge as close to you as they can get, despite the fact that you have the right of way. When they do deign to stop, it is often on the crossing, rather than before it, forcing people to walk around them. Many drivers will not stop to let a pedestrian cross, even if a red light or traffic is preventing them from advancing anyway.

FLYING

Traditionally, the cost of flights was hugely prohibitive for most Romanians. This began to change when first Bucharest and then other cities became part of the network of low-cost flights that now exist. While many younger Romanians are now used to jetting around Europe for work, holidays, and visiting friends living abroad, some members of the older and less affluent generation only headed out of their country for the first time in recent years, typically to visit emigrant adult children. As a result, some Romanians you share planes with may still be relatively new to flying, which can lead to faux pas such as standing immediately behind the person being seen by the passport official rather than behind the painted line, leaping up to retrieve bags from the overhead lockers while the plane is still taxiing, trying to use cell phones on board, and general pushing and rushing. This is not deliberate rudeness, so patience and understanding is encouraged. Once settled in their seats and enjoying the in-flight alcohol and coffee, some Romanians can be as open and chatty as they are on other forms of public transportation. Groups of Romanians once generally greeted the successful landing of the plane they were on with a round of applause, although this is becoming less common as the novelty of flying wears off.

HEALTH

No inoculations are currently required to travel to Romania, but it is worth double-checking with your doctor a few weeks before you go. The food is unlikely to present a problem, and while the water is safe to drink, city water can be tainted by old piping, so most people buy bottled or filter it.

The level of most medical treatments you might likely need is fine. Reciprocal agreements with several countries, including EU and EEA states, entitle their nationals to free emergency medical treatment. Holders of a European Health Insurance Card—or for UK nationals post-Brexit, a Global Health Insurance Card (GHIC)—can access state-provided healthcare at a reduced cost or sometimes free. Even if you have to pay, simple procedures at a public hospital, where you should present yourself, are not usually expensive. For others, private health insurance is recommended. There are private clinics that meet international standards, although these tend to be in the big cities, and in rural areas facilities are often lacking. Most medics in the big cities speak English.

As we have seen, stray dogs—a by-product of the mass rehousing of the Communist era—no longer blight cities and towns. But if you do feel threatened by a dog, walk away from it slowly, avoiding eye contact. Exposure to rabies is highly unlikely.

SAFETY

In general, traveling in Romania is safer than in most European countries. Bucharest is far less violent than comparable cities, and muggings are rare. Security guards can be found patrolling (or at least hanging around and smoking at) a range of unlikely places, from empty buildings to small grocery stores. The most trouble you're likely to encounter is of the nonviolent, sneaky kind: pickpocketing and low-level scams aimed at foreigners, most of them perpetrated by the most hapless of would-be con men. Women are more likely to be subjected to low-level hassles. Groups of youths will often play silly pranks when a lone woman walks past, such as shouting loudly to make her jump or jumping in her way to force her to walk around. Younger women may be subjected to inane approaches from men, in the vain hope that this will result in a date. These encounters are seldom dangerous, but can be annoying. If you're walking alone, it's better to cross the street and avoid any dubious-looking groups of males. A persistent admirer may go away if ignored—otherwise, it is better to move on.

If you should have the misfortune to be robbed or scammed, report it to the police. It is unlikely the perpetrator will be apprehended—although the police may be more inclined to act if the victim is foreign or persistent—but you may need the documentation to make an insurance claim.

The other main threat to safety in Romania is traffic: while the situation is improving along with the roads, Romania had the highest traffic mortality rate in the EU in 2024. Erratic and aggressive drivers, old Dacias with substandard brakes in more disadvantaged areas, and the lack of road sense of some motorists combine to create dangerous chaos on the roads. While traffic in the city centers is likely to be too slow-moving for accidents to be serious, many intercity highways lack median strips, and the two opposing high-speed lanes of traffic see frequent fatal crashes.

CHAPTER **EIGHT**

BUSINESS BRIEFING

THE CHANGING ECONOMY

The Communist economies of Eastern Europe were rife with inefficiencies, injustices, and abuses. Romania's economy suffered the further burden of Ceauşescu's drive to pay off the national debt by exporting the bulk of production, leaving the country criminally short of basic necessities. Romanians had a saying, comparing the state of their country during and after Communism: "Then, we had money but there was nothing in the shops to buy. Now the shops are full and we have no money to buy anything with."

Today—the momentum-sapping effect of the global economic crisis and pandemic notwithstanding—the outlook has been transformed. The economy grew rapidly up until 2008 thanks to foreign investment and the vote of confidence that came with EU accession; and while it has been buffeted by external shocks and domestic deficiencies, it has rebounded well. The privatization of formerly state-owned, often loss-making companies, and the entrance of multinational corporations, have raised local standards and services and seen wages soar. In turn, the rising salaries have helped stem the brain drain: while previously, ambitious professionals often sought their fortune abroad, white-collar workers can now attain a desirable lifestyle at home, and there's a dynamic startup and entrepreneurial scene.

IT, including outsourcing, has been a shining star of the economy, in cities like Cluj as well as in Bucharest. Another boom area has been real estate (although the collapse of the local property market from 2008 left many homeowners burned). Because the majority of urban Romanians live in grim Communist-era apartments, developers have seen their rising purchasing power as an opportunity. Malls, office buildings, and logistics facilities have also been popping up all over the country. The general dearth of services, infrastructure, and businesses before the revolution has led to similar growth across the economy. Young people's language skills and the country's position by the Black Sea are further pulls for foreign companies—although rising wages have seen some business models based on low labor costs switch their focus to Asian countries.

Despite this buoyancy, there are concerns. The recovery has been driven mainly by domestic consumption and exports, raising questions over sustainability and leaving the economy vulnerable. Many deep-rooted issues remain unaddressed: low productivity (despite the fact that Romanians work some of the longest hours in the EU—38.8 a week according to research from 2024); inadequate competitiveness and "value added production;" and investors' difficulty in finding well-trained people in some areas.

THE DACIA

The flagship product of the old Communist economy was the Dacia car. Despite its obvious deficiencies, Romanians took great pride in the odd-looking vehicle, which in its heyday had long waiting lists, and it remains one of the country's most loved brands (at least among the patriotic). The transformation of the Dacia is also a good illustration of the development of the economy at large. The original inferior plant, hampered by a lack of modern technology, was bought in 1999 by Renault, who invested heavily in it. Models of the vehicle quickly improved, and recent versions have sold well and are now exported to the West. In 2010, Dacia launched its first SUV, the Duster, while 2021 saw the introduction of the Spring, one of Europe's cheapest electric vehicles. The company is now taken seriously as a European carmaker.

Challenges notwithstanding, the Romanian market remains an exciting and hotly tipped one. Rising living standards are making the country—more specifically, the capital and big cities—an enjoyable place for foreign executives to work in. And while Western entrepreneurialism is closer to the saturation point, in Romania it is still possible to come up with a new idea and make a success of it.

BUSINESS CULTURE

While Romania was once considered something of a "Wild East," the business environment is becoming more equitable and stable. This is largely due to EU intervention, as well as pressure from lobbyist groups such as the Foreign Investors Council. Although the corporate world is aligning itself with Western practices, however, this is still a country in transition, and unpredictable things happen.

Degrees of Formality

Romanian companies, particularly state-run or locally managed ones, traditionally embraced formality. Suits were worn, meetings scheduled far in advance, handshakes and business cards exchanged, and protocol followed strictly. This level of decorum continued until you got to know your associates better, after which they may have relaxed things. Now, however, unless you are dealing with the most old-school or provincial of businesspeople, proceedings are far less rigid. In multinational firms and less formal businesses, such as media or IT, where the staff tends to be young, things are very different. The uniform here is more likely to be jeans and sneakers, employees may put up posters, and there is a high degree of informality among the staff.

Unless you are certain of your audience, do not try to use humor to set people at ease in negotiations, as it does not always travel. Avoid irony with new acquaintances; people may not detect it, and may interpret light-hearted self-deprecation as a genuine admission of weakness.

Working Practices

Traditional business hours are from 9:00 a.m. to 5:00 p.m., but nowadays there is more flexibility; many people stay in the office until later in the evening, and may invite you for meetings up to around 8:00 p.m., while emails may be sent late into the night. While some employees do devote much of their lives to their work, the culture of work avoidance that grew up under Communism, when there was no incentive to be productive, may still be encountered. Until fairly recently, employees did not typically enjoy much leeway regarding when they worked; however, the rise in remote working occasioned by the pandemic, and legislative efforts to support working parents, have led to greater work schedule flexibility. The decampment of manual workers westwards for better salaries has left a dearth on the local market; if you find a tradesperson who returns your calls, turns up on time, and actually fixes the problem, you have found the holy grail.

BRIBERY AND CORRUPTION

Romania's history of corruption predates the Communist regime—although, needless to say, that didn't improve matters. The country has traditionally ranked far down the transparency league tables, and has long been considered among the most corrupt in Europe. The Microsoft licensing scandal, in which seven former ministers narrowly escaped jail in 2018 after the government accepted $50 million in bribes to approve increases in license fees for Microsoft products, and the Nordis pyramid scheme, which emerged in 2023, with apartments sold to multiple buyers and down payments taken for homes that were never built, reportedly defrauding would-be homeowners of over $200 million, are two of the most egregious cases.

The victim of much of the corruption is the state—that is, the Romanian people. State officials are often poorly paid and retain a Communist mentality. A typical example of corruption might see a company pay a bribe to ensure it wins a government tender, with a million-euro cut going to the officials who facilitate the deal. Of course, another company could often have performed the work better, and for less money. The result of this is a few state paper pushers who earn, in theory, a modest salary but live in huge villas, plus a substandard and costly white elephant project foisted on the public and a large dent in the state coffers. Businesses pay bribes to middlemen and facilitators, without which there is precious little chance of the deal going through.

The increasing use of online processes, the arrival of international companies—with their Western standards, relative transparency, and codes of ethics—and some high-profile prosecutions have helped to change things significantly. Many of the younger generation are thoroughly frustrated with the corruption, and bring a modern, more ethical attitude to their dealings. This is partly fueled by their ability to travel; whereas their parents' generation knew only the local reality, they have seen how business is conducted abroad. The country's EU aspirations were also a spur to clamping down on graft, and the strict EU monitoring process has made it more difficult to get away with nefarious practices. This is not to say that Romania is now corruption-free (particularly not the state sector); but as younger, more open-minded, and more optimistic people take over from the old guard, it is on the right track, and corruption is certainly less visible on a day-to-day level.

Part of the reason that dishonesty flourished was Romania's passive civil society. Older people were conditioned to graft, and the oppressive and brutal governments of the past stamped out any public inclination to protest. The emergence of NGOs, however, has been a positive force, with many groups calling attention to corruption and pressing for action against it, and protesters marching en masse against graft on several occasions.

CONNECTIONS

While multinational companies in Romania operate much as they do elsewhere, in smaller firms connections and personal relationships take on great significance. In all walks of life, not just business, Romanians have difficulty trusting strangers. Friends, lovers, business partners, lawyers, and accountants may all be chosen from within a close-knit social circle. The thinking seems to be, "Better the devil you know," while Romania's status as a "particularistic" culture (in cross-cultural researcher Fons Trompenaars' framework) sees it value personal relationships over impersonal rules and processes. As a result, connections in business are vital.

A Romanian business partner will have to learn to trust you before doing business with you, and it can take time to build up this relationship. An introduction from a mutual contact will certainly help. If you are negotiating on behalf of your company, your Romanian associates will consider the relationship to be with you rather than your firm. If you have to be replaced, the process of trust building has to start over. In this situation, try to introduce your replacement to your associates.

This value placed on connections means that when hiring staff, some Romanian bosses look far more favorably on applicants recommended by people they know—Romanians can be vengeful, and managers fear a disgruntled ex-employee subsequently getting them in trouble with the authorities for some minor violation. A foreigner first arriving in Romania and not knowing anyone may initially find it difficult to get work.

BUREAUCRACY

Romania is still burdened with a spirit-crushing bureaucracy. The simplest task, which should take a few minutes, can drag on interminably.

The most bureaucratic institutions tend to belong to the state. Operating hours, procedures, and attitudes can leave a lot to be desired. Businesspeople decry Romania's tax and accounting system as complex and unfriendly to small firms, with monthly tax declarations, frequent rule changes—and indeed, entire policy changes—and a tax authority (ANAF) that whacks disproportionate fines on minor errors.

The main victims of this are entrepreneurs. Large companies can afford to send employees or hire consultants to stand in line all day to get whatever document is required, but the small business owner will find that an awful lot of time gets eaten up in the performance of such tedious necessities. The online payment of taxes and bills, and greater use of IT, has helped in places. But greater digitization has caused its own problems: some say the rollout of mandatory electronic invoicing system e-Factura, with its pre-approved Romanian providers, and lack of user friendliness and guidance, has in fact made a bad system worse and processes longer. EU-led efforts to reduce the gray economy have met some local resistance and administrative blockages as local institutions struggle with new procedures.

The Bureaucracy Industry

The symbol of bureaucracy in Romania was the stamp, needed for a vast range of official documents in various aspects of business and civic life. While greater digitalization has heralded the end of the stamp's reign, Romania's bureaucracy still has its own flourishing industry—shops called *ştampile expres* (stamps express) all over the place, selling stamps and the other paraphernalia of bureaucracy.

Fortunately, the multinational companies in Romania have helped change things. They typically started off with foreign country managers, who trained their workforce in Western business practices, before handing the reins over to local replacements. While these companies have little influence over the state bureaucracy, at least their own procedures are less cumbersome and fairly similar to the international norm.

THE BLACK MARKET

Under Communism, Kent cigarettes served as a second currency and were exchanged for much-needed goods. The period had a profound effect on the public mentality, and much black market activity continued unabated even after independence.

Cigarette smuggling persists, though counterfeit designer clothing and alcoholic spirits are less common than they were. The main piracy area now is computers and the internet: the former president, Traian Basescu, once told Bill Gates that digital pirating had helped Romania's software industry flourish. Research from 2023 suggested that 53% of all installed software in Romania is pirated, although these days this is more at an individual level, rather than also in offices. Growing incomes and the advent of affordable streaming platforms like Netflix, Spotify, and so on mean that most Romanians now find it more convenient to consume content legitimately, rather than via torrents—although tech-savvy, cash-poor youngsters do still use them to access expensive video games.

THE LEGAL SYSTEM

Romania's legal system is modeled on the French Napoleonic Code. Trials are normally conducted in public, although there are exceptions in extenuating circumstances. At times, Romania's courts have resembled those in Charles Dickens's novel *Bleak House*. Cases can drag on almost indefinitely, with little hope of an equitable outcome. While political pressure is still exerted in high-profile cases, corruption among judges is less common these days. What remains a problem is the number and competence of judges: with too few magistrates for the rising court case count, lawyers complain that judgments are rushed and lacking in merit, as judges are not sufficiently well trained to understand more complex cases. Meanwhile, the legislation is lacking and subject to frequent changes, most of which fail to deliver improvements. This unpredictable legal environment deters potential investors, and many people with legitimate grievances let them drop rather than face the probably futile challenge of trying to get redress through the courts.

Some entrepreneurs also complain that employment law favors workers, making it difficult to sack people, although this may depend on one's national origin: while Americans may see the local framework as restrictive, others say the law favors employers more than in some Western European countries. Multinationals sometimes manage to reconcile their global processes with Romanian rules. Labor legislation is formal: a small, technical mistake in layoff paperwork can have significant ramifications.

BUSINESS HIERARCHIES

Traditionally, Romanian society was rigidly hierarchical, with age, title, and position all highly respected. Even today, in state institutions and traditional firms at least, seniority and wisdom gained over time are often the key factors in the decision-making process, and the final say falls to the highest-ranking person. Promotions, too, may be awarded based on length of service in the company, rather than talent. This can be frustrating for young, dynamic employees whose abilities go unrecognized. However, multinational corporations, or local firms run on international principles, are now becoming more common, and they are much more likely to reward individual talent and potential.

A similar difference can be observed in levels of formality. While in more modern or Western-style companies it is common for a new employee to use first names for everybody, up to and including the boss, in traditional Romanian companies or public sector workplaces people are sometimes expected to start by using a person's title and surname, or sometimes title and first name, until invited to use their first name only. The immediate use of first names would be presumptuous, although as usual there is some leeway for foreigners. Romanians may talk to subordinates in a curt way that sounds quite impolite to an outsider; equally, they may adopt a deferential tone to a superior.

GROUPTHINK

Given that until fairly recently, independent thought was useless if not dangerous, it is little surprise that many people are far more comfortable following orders than using their own initiative to solve problems. Another factor is the education system, which has traditionally emphasized rote learning at the expense of creativity. This can manifest in a lack of initiative, or a reluctance to depart from established ways of doing things. However, with the advent of international business education, such as MBAs, this is changing, especially in the private sector, and local businesspeople are also becoming more flexible and better at listening to what the other party needs.

PASSING THE BUCK

Self-deprecation, apologizing, and admission of failure or weakness are not strong points in Romania, where saving face is often a priority. Workplace culture previously came down hard on errant employees, some of whom were simply fined or had their pay docked for mistakes, rather than offered extra training or advice to correct the problem. This is rare now, but there is still a culture of buck-passing. Rather than being welcomed as a token of honesty, courage, and responsibility, accepting fault for one's mistake can interpreted as weakness.

RENEGOTIABILITY

The concept of negotiability in Romania is elastic. Whereas usually a price being negotiable means the seller may consider reducing it slightly, in Romania an agreed-upon price could just as easily be subsequently negotiated upward by the seller, if he or she decides that the market value has risen, gets a better offer, or just feels like it. The fluctuating market, lack of business ethics, and still-developing legal system are all factors in this "Wild East" mentality and behavior. When doing business, it is wise not to assume that any deal is done until all the contracts are signed—and even then things can change, as we will see.

"YES" BECOMES "NO"

An irritating phenomenon for foreigners is the habit some Romanians have of entering into negotiations, taking them to an advanced stage, making an apparent agreement, and then pulling out at the last minute or simply ghosting you. This can partly be explained by the Romanian propensity for telling people what they want to hear rather than the truth: instead of telling you "no," the person prefers to procrastinate and defer until it becomes obvious they have no intention of proceeding. This usually happens after protracted negotiations, in which the other party started out highly enthusiastic to do business as soon as possible.

Sometimes this is because they are using your offer to bargain down another party. Another possible explanation is that Latin pride makes people reluctant to admit that they cannot afford the fee being asked for. Lower-ranked workers may not be granted much authority or allowed to use their own initiative, and decisions often have to be approved at different levels, so it could also be the case that a project one person proposes may be rejected by a higher-up. In any event, to avoid frustration, it is better not to assume things are definite until you have signed on the dotted line.

WOMEN IN BUSINESS

Despite the sexism rife in Romanian society, the business world offers something closer to parity. Communism encouraged women to seek employment—while still being left with child-rearing and domestic duties—and they are well represented in the workforce, although fewer reach the higher echelons of business or politics.

As elsewhere, the "female professions," such as teaching, nursing, and clerical work, tend to be lower paid than "male professions," such as construction, and the gender wage gap is 20 percent, according to PwC research from 2025. Although there is legislation that theoretically guarantees equal treatment at work, some female employees and entrepreneurs still suffer from chauvinistic attitudes. As is common in Romania, nationality trumps gender, and a Western female expatriate is unlikely to experience much in the way of workplace sexism directly.

MEETINGS

On the Day

Turn up on time. Romanians value punctuality, while not always adhering to it themselves—you may have to wait. If your counterparts do not speak English—though this is vanishingly rare in the business world, especially in Bucharest—take your own interpreter; this is something you can check in advance. In the past, meetings tended to be formal, with business suits the expected attire, but this is less often the case these days, especially in the creative domains. Shake hands firmly, meeting the other person's gaze. Business cards, where they have not been supplanted by digital alternatives, are exchanged early on. Include the date your company was founded if it has a long history, as stability can impress Romanians.

More traditional people may indicate where you should sit; younger ones will probably be more relaxed about this. Meetings tend to be warm, with drinks and snacks provided. This is not an invitation to relax totally, however; old-fashioned courtesy is the norm. Proceedings will probably be dominated by the most senior person present, who has the responsibility for all major decisions; save any of your concessions for this discussion. Romanians may negotiate toughly. Communicate directly, but sensitively, and do not use the hard sell. While there may be an agenda, this will not be adhered to rigidly. Interruption is a common element of conversation in Romania, but show respect to senior participants.

Presentations

Romanians are impressed by appearances; presenting your report on a laptop, and dressing it up with the latest software and other trappings, is a good start. That said, it should still be thoroughly researched and with plenty of facts. Romanian audiences are likely to listen to your presentation politely, without interrupting, although it is advisable to keep it short and to the point.

CONTRACTS AND THEIR FULFILLMENT

Contracts play a significant role in Romanian business, even for small matters where they would not be considered necessary elsewhere. They may be subject to repeated revision, especially if circumstances change; and they must be registered with the relevant authority, and therefore need to be in the local language. Certain offices are licensed to give official translations (*traduceri autorizate*), but be prepared for their proficiency in the foreign language to be lower than you might expect. Business contracts are usually shorter than in the US or UK, for example, since most of the general rules governing a type of contract are provided by the legislation, eliminating the need to reproduce them in the contract.

Once a contract is signed, maintain contact to check that things are progressing appropriately. Most Romanians respond best to clear leadership, rather than being left to figure things out on their own. Disputes tend to be settled out of court by lawyers, as neither party wants to enter the chronically understaffed legal system, which involves frequent delays and postponements. Legislation is not always business-friendly, and while the country has been clamping down on corruption and political interference in the judiciary, these problems remain. Some businesspeople complain of partners negotiating a low price based on the promise of high sales volumes, then ordering smaller quantities.

CHAPTER **NINE**

COMMUNICATING

DIRECTNESS

We have seen that Romanians are a straight-talking people whose directness can sometimes faze foreign visitors. A perfectly unemotional conversation can sound so loud and brusque that it appears to be a heated argument. It is quite common for people, either within a family or in a work situation, to issue a series of orders to each other, none of which will be prefaced with the equivalent of "can you" or "would you mind." They argue, logically, that such phrases could imply that the other person has the right to refuse.

In social settings, the majority of these orders will simply be ignored by Romanians as background noise, but a foreign visitor not aware of the phenomenon may be taken aback by a sudden series of directions on where to sit, what to eat, what to drink, and how to do

A young couple enjoying an outdoor lunch in the Bucharest city center.

it. In an office environment, the orders will be carried out without the subordinate feeling that they have been spoken to discourteously.

Ps and Qs

Because Romanians consider the essence of the message to be more important than how it is dressed up, conversation is punctuated with fewer polite phrases than you may be used to. Orders and requests will often be stated without a "please" (*vă rog* or *te rog*), and people may be served food and drink, at home or out, without feeling the need to thank the server. As with many similar customs, this is not intended as rudeness; it is possibly the outcome of an unfussy rural culture, or a straight-to-the-point communication style. Romanians are surprised by the number of "pleases" and "thank yous" that foreigners can fit into a short exchange, and many consider them quite unnecessary.

GHOSTING

The inefficient, distorted commerce that took place under Communism did not allow normal business etiquette to develop. This has many manifestations, but perhaps one of the most annoying for foreigners is people's tendency to ignore emails and phone calls.

Employees, even in multinational companies, may not reply to important messages or fail to phone back. This usually results in your having to chase them, in which case only a minority will apologize for their omission—the majority will not consider that they have done anything wrong. This is to some extent understandable if you are calling for a reason that benefits you (for example, to chase down payment), but wholly unfathomable when the person whose call or mail you are waiting for stands to benefit from replying (for example, when you are a customer). You are more likely to be ghosted when you're cold calling than when contacting someone with whom you've previously dealt, another example of the central role of personal relationships.

MAIL

Step inside a Romanian post office and you could almost be back in the Communist era. Although some have been renovated, most are dreary places, staffed largely by women on some of the lowest salaries in the country.

When negotiating the frustratingly bureaucratic postal system, it is quite usual to be directed from one post office to another for the simple task of, say, sending a package by registered post. As well as dealing with mail, post offices are also an option for bill payment (although today consumers also have bank and online alternatives). Occasionally long lines build up, and windows can be closed quite peremptorily. Fortunately the service, once you can access it, is usually reliable, with airmail reaching Western Europe in around a week. In Bucharest, most larger post offices are open from 8:00 a.m. to 8:00 p.m. on Monday to Friday and from 8:00 a.m. to 2:00 p.m. on Saturday. Outside the capital, especially in more rural areas, weekday hours are usually from 9.30 a.m. to

One of the iconic red letterboxes of the Romanian postal system.

5:00 p.m. Post offices have a red sign displaying the Poşta Romấna logo, a red background with a yellow "RO" on it and a horn in the colors of the Romanian flag. Ordering goods from outside the EU can be quite an adventure, with long waiting times for the delivery and several bureaucratic hurdles.

TELEPHONES

Landlines (known locally as fixed phones) are an extremely rare sight outside of offices, and have even sometimes been dispensed with inside offices, killed off by rock-bottom cell phone rates. Smartphones are near ubiquitous.

Phone users may notice an interesting phenomenon when a caller has dialed the wrong number. In response to your opening "Hello" (or "*Alo*" in Romanian), the caller, rather than ask for the person they want, or state their name or purpose, will generally reply "*Alo*?", leaving you with little option other than to repeat "*Alo*" yourself. They will then often inquire, quite assertively, who you are (conveying some indignation that you are not the person they expected you to be), with no notion that as the caller, the onus is on them to introduce themselves. On other occasions, a caller who has dialed the wrong number will simply hang up when they realize their mistake, with no apology for disturbing you. While this can seem rude, it stems more from the logical view that both parties' time will be wasted by continuing the conversation.

CELL PHONES AND SIM CARDS

Cell phones have caught on in a big way in Romania. Mobile phone penetration as a percentage of the population is over 100 percent according to the World Bank, with over four out of five people owning a smartphone, and many owning two. A young person without a smartphone is virtually unthinkable, even in rural areas. Even older people use the technology, typically encouraged by their children. Orange, Vodafone, and RCS & RDS/Digi are the main service

Two friends checking their phones while parking their rental scooters, Coltea Park, Bucharest.

providers. Traditionally, richer customers tended to have contracts, paid for with a monthly bill, while the less well off, including a lot of students, had prepay deals, where they paid to put credit on their phones in advance. However, greater affordability as tariffs have been forced down by competition has made postpay contracts more widely affordable. WhatsApp is very popular as a way to keep in touch and make arrangements, as are other online platforms.

An interesting phenomenon in the early days of rapid mobile phone expansion was "the beep." People who had less money would call the person they wished to speak to, hanging up before the phone could be answered. That person was expected to phone them back, and so foot the cost of the call. While some people considered the beep rather cheap and cheeky, others saw it as a way of allowing poorer people—particularly those on prepay deals where the cost of calls was high—to stay in touch; and if you accidentally answered a call that was meant to be a beep, you were often greeted by a rather disgruntled caller. However, with the advent of cheaper contracts with plenty of minutes included, plus online voice apps like WhatsApp, the beep has been consigned to telephonic history.

There are few social restrictions on where a cell phone can be used. Drivers often talk holding their phone while behind the wheel, even though this is illegal. Few people would consider it bad manners to make or receive a call while eating in a restaurant. Cell phones frequently ring in the cinema, and while some people will go outside to answer the call, many will conduct their conversation in the auditorium during the film. Although it is rarer, the same can happen at a live event such as a classical music concert.

THE INTERNET

Romanians have eagerly embraced the internet, both for work and particularly for leisure. They quickly adopted chat rooms and then social media, and most people—aside, perhaps, from the elderly—have email, with Gmail a popular provider. Facebook and YouTube are among the destinations, while TikTok and Instagram have rapidly gained ground among younger demographics.

Home access was boosted by increasing wages and instituting government programs to facilitate computer ownership among poor families. Internet connection is usually through one of the main cable TV firms, RCS & RDS/Digi, Orange, and Vodafone. The smartphone boom means most consumers enjoy access to 5G mobile broadband. Romanians are proud to tell you that their country has some of the fastest Internet speeds in not only Europe but the world, a fact that US presidential hopeful Bernie Sanders caused a local stir about by tweeting on the subject in 2016. Free Wi-Fi access is common in restaurants, malls, cafes, and other public spaces.

THE MEDIA

From its propaganda-fueled days under Communism, the media has faced an uphill battle to become professional, independent, and fit for purpose.

We have seen that television has traditionally been the main medium in terms of influence, share of advertising (52 percent in 2025), and adoption. Digital's advertising share of 36 percent, radio at 5 percent, and print below 1 percent gives a fair idea of the sway of the respective formats—although more Romanians now get their news online than from the TV, the latter still shapes opinion more. As elsewhere, newspaper circulations have dwindled and print versions of papers have been shuttered and shifted online, while radio plays a background role.

A handful of major conglomerates dominate the television landscape, and political or business interests are often blatant in their influence. Viewers tend to be loyal to the channels that reflect (and mold) their outlook, and it's important to know the agenda of the channel you're watching to be able to gauge the output. The state-run service is Televiziunea Română (TVR), which relies on advertising sales since the license fee was abolished in 2017, weakening its already disputed editorial independence. The top two private stations, Antena 1 and Pro TV, attract higher audiences. There is no national channel in English, but because most people have cable there are plenty of international options, and much local output consists of subtitled American imports. News programs feature car accidents and salacious gossip alongside hard news.

The newspaper sector is largely tabloid, with the market leader a lowbrow daily called *Click!* followed by the formerly downmarket *Libertatea*, which has attempted to raise its game and tackle more serious subjects over the last decade. Business paper *Ziarul Financiar* is the only one of quality, while *Adevãrul* and *Evenimentul Zilei* are somewhere between tabloid and mainstream. Online outlets G4media, Hotnews, Recorder, Context, and Euronews (the latter also having a TV station), where younger, middle-class Romanians get their news and analysis, also conduct investigations into high-level corruption. Specialist sites, such as Edupedu and Scoala 9, covering education, and Scena9, reporting on the arts and culture, offer quality journalism. Bloggers have a rising role in the mediascape, alongside social media platforms—the clout of the latter was in evidence when a viral TikTok campaign catapulted Călin Georgescu from nowhere into the (subsequently cancelled) second round of the 2024 presidential election.

Parts of the media—particularly the TV scene—are still blighted by a lack of independence, transparency, and professionalism. The tone of coverage can be partisan and, at times, conspiratorial. Some outlets routinely blur the lines between reporting and opinion, or between journalism and propaganda. The result is that just 27 percent of Romanians trust the news, putting the country forty-fourth out of forty-seven markets surveyed by the Reuters Institute Digital News Report 2025, a ranking in keeping with the Romanian tendency toward skepticism. Clickbait and inflammatory headlines abound, reflecting both the commercial pressures on outlets and the public's appetite for scandal. There are a few honorable exceptions, one such being investigative journalist Cătălin Tolontan, whose exposé of the medical system corruption that contributed to the deaths of young clubgoers after the 2015 Colectiv fire formed part of a documentary that became the first Romanian film to be nominated for an Academy Award. He typifies a small but resilient cluster of independent platforms that produce rigorous, impactful reporting, though often with limited resources. The website *Times New Roman*, a Romanian take on *The Onion*, also throws punches at the powerful.

In practice, foreigners typically interact little with Romanian media. The internet (with help from the pandemic) has pretty much killed off the print magazines and listings guides that catered to English speakers. They have been succeeded by a wealth of online resources for foreigners, with websites and Facebook pages covering everything from general news and what's on (Romania Insider, Universul.net, Go Visit Bucharest), to groups and communities (British people in Romania, or foreigners in Bucharest, for example), and specific interests (activities in Bucharest for children, business groups like Dynamic Business Connections, etc.).

CONCLUSION

If you have made it this far undeterred by what you have read, you are probably the kind of visitor who could get a lot out of traveling in Romania. Life doesn't always unfold smoothly, but the rewards far outweigh the irritations.

The aim of this book is not only to prepare you for some of the frustrations you might face, but also to set out the liberating, exciting, and heartwarming aspects of Romanian life. In a fast-developing country, tangible changes are visible even in a short stay, buoyed by the people's hope that this time things may be better.

Despite the many setbacks and deprivations they have suffered, the Romanians remain warm and welcoming, and not even limited means can stop them from being the most generous hosts. Guests in Romania are never regarded as a nuisance, and as a visitor to their homeland you have privileged status; people will go out of their way to assist you, seldom with any motive other than to help a stranger in a foreign land and create a good impression of their country. This is just one of the national characteristics that will put all the fading Communist hangovers in perspective. Romania's faults are well documented; its many endearments still await discovery.

FURTHER READING

Blacker, William. *Along the Enchanted Way: A Story of Love and Life in Romania*. John Murray Publishers Ltd, 2010.

Deletant, Dennis. *Romania Under Communist Rule*. London: Center for Romanian Studies, 1999.

Djuvara, Neagu. *A Brief Illustrated History of Romanians*. Humanitas, 2021.

Gallagher, Tom. *Modern Romania: The End of Communism, the Failure of Democratic Reform, and the Theft of a Nation*. New York: New York University Press, 2005.

Georgescu, Irina. *Carpathia: Food from the Heart of Romania*. Northampton: Interlink Publishers, 2024.

Eminescu, Mihai (translated by Leon Levitchi and Andrei Bantas). *Poezii / Poems*. Teora, 1999.

Humphreys, C.C.. *Vlad: The Last Confession*. Orion, 2009.

Kenyon, Paul. *Children of the Night: The Strange and Epic Story of Modern Romania*. New York: Apollo Publishers, 2023.

Klepper, Nicolae. *Taste of Romania: Its Cookery and Glimpses of Its History, Folklore, Art, Literature, and Poetry*. New York: Hippocrene Books, expanded edition 1999.

Mandache, Diana. *Later Chapters of My Life: The Lost Memoir of Queen Marie of Romania*. Gloucestershire, UK: Sutton Publishing, 2004.

Manea, Norman. *The Hooligan's Return: A Memoir*. New York: Farrar, Straus and Giroux, 2003.

Manning, Olivia. *The Balkan Trilogy*. Arrow Books, 1960.

Müller, Herta (translated by Michael Hofmann). *The Land of Green Plums*. Granta Books, 1999.

Pacepa, Ion Mihai. *Red Horizons: The True Story of Nicolae and Elena Ceausescu's Crimes, Lifestyle, and Corruption*. Washington, D.C.: Regnery Publishing, Inc., 1990.

Pralong, Sandra (editor). *More Romanian than the Romanians? Why foreigners fall in love with Romania*. Polirom, 2013.

Sepetys, Ruta. *I Must Betray You*. Philomel Books, 2022.

Siani-Davies, Peter. *The Romanian Revolution of December 1989*. New York: Cornell University Press, 2005.

USEFUL APPS

Travel and Transportation

Bolt, **Uber**, and **Blue** offer ride-share services in Romania, while **StarTaxi** lets you book a traditional taxi (it also accepts online payments).

The national railway app **CFR Călători** provides information on train schedules and services. You can also book tickets on the app.

InfoTB offers real-time public transport information in Bucharest, including route planning and live tracking of buses and trams. **CityMapper** and **Google Maps** are popular navigation apps locally.

Passengers can pay for travel on buses and trams via **24Pay**.

Pay for street parking in cities using **AmParcat**.

Food and Shopping

Bolt Food, **Glovo**, and **Wolt** offer restaurant delivery in Romania's main cities, while **Bringo**, **Freshful**, **Seasamo**, and **Carrefour** deliver groceries and other household items.

Both **Revolut** and **Wise** are commonly used for sending and receiving money, alongside local banks' apps.

eMAG (a local version of Amazon) is the biggest online marketplace, while **Altex** and **Flanco** are electronics retailers. In the secondhand domain, **OLX** is the local eBay equivalent, while fashion site **Vinted** is also popular.

Socializing and Communication

WhatsApp and **Facebook** are both popular messaging platforms locally, while **DuoLingo** and **Google Translate** are your friends when you communicate with non-English speakers.

PICTURE CREDITS

Cover image: *Aerial view of the Old Town, Brasov, Transylvania, Romania.* © Adobe Stock

Shutterstock: 12 by ANAND RAVEENDRAN, 14 by Calin Stan, 35 by LCV, 44 by Dragos Asaftei, 45 by Gaspar Janos; 46, 79 by ecstk22; 63 by Balate.Dorin, 76 by Cristi Croitoru, 80 by Gabriel.F, 81 by Gabriel Preda RO, 84 by CornelPutan, 85 by mikkeell, 87 by VIS Fine Art, 88 by 997Cata, 91 by Whiteaster, 97 by Angela Cini, 106 by Cristi Croitoru, 111 by Nomad Pixel, 113 by Elena M. Tarasova, 122 by ELEPHOTOS, 128 by Angela Cini, 132 by Fotokon, 141 by Dragos Asaftei, 146 by Balate.Dorin, 148 by Wirestock Creators, 152 by Dan Gabriel Atanasie, 155 by Sundry Photography, 162 by Stelian Popa, 182 by Remus Rigo, 184 by Cristi Croitoru, 186 by DirkVG, 188 by Sergiy Palamarchuk.

Unsplash: 103 by Stoica Maria.

Creative Commons Attribution-Share Alike 4.0 International 19 by Banekondic1996.

Public Domain: 21, 24, 34.

Romanian Communism Online Photo Collection (Fototeca online a comunismului românesc): 29 (Photo no. #E594).

INDEX

Acknowledgments

This edition is dedicated to the inimitable Ollie and his Grandma. I would like to thank Sinéad Moore, Tony Fekete, Dean Edgar, and Andy Taylor for their contributions to this edition; the members of the British and expat communities who kindly responded to my queries; and Alex and Vasile.